ORDNANCE SURVEY LEISURE GUIDE

PEAK DISTRICT

▲ Harborough Rocks, Brassington

Produced jointly by the Publishing Division of
The Automobile Association and the Ordnance Survey

Consultant for the Peak National Park: Roland Smith, Head of Information Services

Editorial contributors: Roy Christian MBE (A to Z Gazetteer and Gazetteer revisions for the new edition); Clarence Daniel (Peakland Customs); Dr Trevor Elkington (Wildlife of the Peak); Roger Flindall (Lead Mining in the Peak); Mark Richards (Tours and Walks); Ken Smith (Man and the Landscape); Roland Smith (The Story of a National Park, A Day in the Life of a Ranger and the Gazetteer short features); Rebecca Snelling (Fact File).

Original photography: Malc Birkett and Andy Tryner

Phototypeset by Wyvern Typesetting, Bristol
Colour separation by Fotographics Ltd.
Printed and bound by BPC   Paulton Books Ltd.

Maps extracted from the Ordnance Survey's 1:63 360 Tourist Series, 1:25 000 Pathfinder Series and 1:250 000 Routemaster Series with the permission of Her Majesty's Stationery Office. Crown copyright.

Additions to the maps by the Cartographic Department of The Automobile Association and the Ordnance Survey.

Produced by the Publishing Division of The Automobile Association.

Distributed in the United Kingdom by the Ordnance Survey, Southampton, and the Publishing Division of The Automobile Association, Norfolk House, Priestley Road, Basingstoke, Hampshire RG24 9NY.

First edition 1987
Reprinted with amendments 1990
Revised edition 1992
Reprinted 1993, 1994

A CIP catalogue record of this book is available from the British Library.

AA ISBN 0 7495 0386 6 (hardback)
AA ISBN 0 7495 0376 9 (softback)
OS ISBN 0 319 00290 X (hardback)
OS ISBN 0 319 00281 0 (softback)

Published by The Automobile Association and the Ordnance Survey.

Introduction: Lea Gardens

Contents

▲ Carsington

Introduction **5**

Man and the Landscape **6**

The Story of a National Park **10**

Wildlife of the Peak **15**

Lead Mining in the Peak **19**

Peakland Customs **23**

A Day in the Life of a Ranger **27**

A to Z Gazetteer **32**   Fact File **70**

Atlas **77**   Motor Tours **96**

Walks in the Peak District **102**

Index **118**

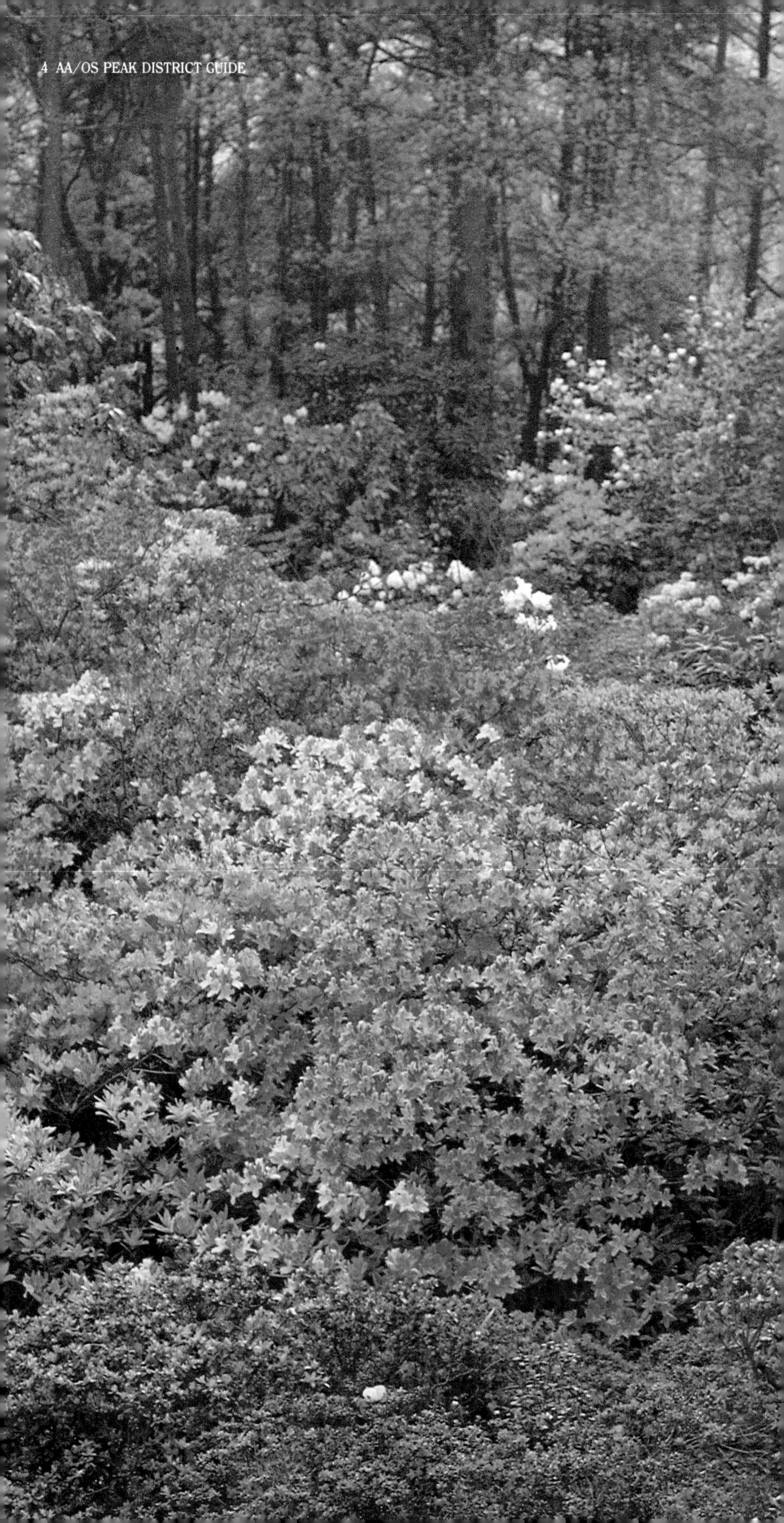

Introduction

For centuries seekers after fortune have been lured to
the Peak District by promises of mineral wealth –
lead ore, Blue John and the decorative Ashford
marble. Ironically, those diligent searchers missed the
greatest treasure of all – the richly-varied landscape
beneath which they worked. Within a huge horseshoe
of stern gritstone – the Dark Peak – lie the pastoral
summits and slopes of the limestone White Peak,
laced with rivers sparkling through deep dales. Great
houses stand in parkland on the banks of the Wye, a
world of caves and mines lies deep in the ground and
all around are legacies of an industrial past. Written
by people who live in the Peak, and backed by the
AA's research expertise and the Ordnance Survey's
mapping, this guide is as useful to those who return
to the area year after year as it is to the first-time visitor.

Man and the Landscape

M odern visitors to the Peak District are attracted to the rugged scenery of the gritstone Dark Peak and the more gentle limestone White Peak. Many, particularly walkers in the Dark Peak, are intent on seeing an original wilderness only partially tamed. In fact the Peak District landscape, even at its most remote, is largely man-made. It abounds with evidence of human impact, from the profusion of dry-stone walls to the development of the peat cover, in which humans certainly had a hand. Much of what can be seen occurred in the last few centuries, the result of the Agricultural and Industrial

Millstones were cut from the grit bones of the Dark Peak landscape to be turned by White Peak rivers

Revolutions. But the story of human activity in the Peak District began much earlier.

The first visitors to the Peak arrived a quarter of a million years ago. They followed reindeer into what was then tundra south of the glaciers that covered most of north Britain. The only evidence is a flint hand-axe they left behind at Hopton, near Wirksworth. There are a few hints of occasional hunting visits by Neanderthal Man during the Ice Age between 80,000 and 30,000BC, but it is only from around 12,000 and 10,000BC, at the very end of the glacial period, that visits by humans begin to increase. Temporary camps were made in the many caves and rock-shelters in the limestone valleys of the White Peak. Examples include Dowel and Fox Hole; Thor's Cave and Ossum's Cave in the Dove and Manifold valleys; One Ash Rock-Shelter, in Lathkill Dale; and the evocatively-named Old Woman's House Cave, near Taddington. From these sites have come flint artifacts and bones of reindeer, items lost or abandoned by the departing hunters to remain as mute testimony to the skills of these Upper Palaeolithic (Old Stone Age) people.

As the glaciers retreated (around 10,000BC), red deer and roe deer replaced the reindeer of the Ice Age. Hunting bands of humans followed the deer on to their upland summer pastures, particularly in the Dark Peak. Evidence suggests that Middle Stone Age hunters bettered their chances of hunting success by felling trees and burning vegetation, to improve grass growth and encourage their prey to graze in predictable locations. These activities probably assisted the later spread of the blanket bog on the gritstone uplands, because water collected on the ground instead of being taken up by the trees. In this way, even as early as 7,000BC, humans had begun to leave their mark on the landscape.

First farmers

Farming was introduced before 3000BC and spread fairly rapidly. Herding domesticated sheep and cattle, and growing primitive forms of wheat and barley, replaced hunting and gathering as a way of living. Where the outskirts of Buxton stand today were wooden rectangular houses built by these early farmers, and elsewhere earthen long mounds were constructed for their dead. For the first time there was permanent settlement on the limestone plateau where the less dense tree cover and the light soils suited the primitive range of farm tools available.

By 2000BC mass burials were being made in chambers built of enormous stones incorporated into large circular cairns like that at Minninglow, an enormous burial mound which imposes itself, even as a ruin, upon the landscape of the southern Peak. Ceremonial monuments were also built for the first time. The two henges of Abror Low, the 'Stonehenge of the North', with its circle of fallen stones, and the Bull Ring at Dove Holes, appear to oversee separate territories divided by the River Wye. Whether built as markets or fairs, as meeting places or locations for ceremony and ritual, their precise function remains enigmatic.

Bronze Age people settled widely in the White Peak, and dozens of burial mounds dot the limestone hilltops. Over 400 Peak District barrows were excavated by Thomas Bateman, in the middle years of the 19th century (the collection of grave goods accumulated by this energetic Victorian antiquarian is now housed in Sheffield City

Circles in time. The ancient henge monument of Arbor Low is echoed in form by a more recent dew pond

Museum). Apart from barrows, few other remains can be found on the limestone, and the most complete and best preserved remains of Bronze Age settlement are found on Stanton Moor and on the dramatic gritstone edges east of the Derwent, where plentiful remnants have been preserved since about 1000BC by the very inhospitality of these bleak moorlands.

Until recently hill-forts were thought to be a feature of the Iron Age, prior to the Roman occupation. However, work at Mam Tor, near Castleton, now suggests that it was occupied in the early Bronze Age, much earlier than was previously thought possible. Peak District hill-forts may have been a response to social pressures in the later Bronze Age when the gritstone moorlands were being abandoned, rather than a later Iron Age phenomenon. At Harborough Rocks there are hints of Iron Age activity in about 500BC, and an earthwork enclosure on Tideswell Moor is clipped by the later Bathamgate Roman road, allowing it to be dated to the pre-Roman period. But the overall evidence is sparse, perhaps indicating that this was a virtually depopulated border country.

The Romans

This apparent isolation was rudely shattered by the Roman invasion of Britain. In the early 70sAD the Romans moved north from the River Trent and occupied the Peak, primarily to exploit the rich deposits of lead for which the area was known. With customary Roman efficiency, two forts were established, one at Brough (*Navio*) and another on the western fringes of the Peak at *Melandra* (*Ardotalia*), Glossop. A system of roads was constructed surrounding and crossing the Peak, linking the forts with those established at other points around the region.

The centre of Roman lead production is thought to have been *Lutudarum*, which has not been found but was probably in the Wirksworth and

Carsington area. The name has been found on Roman pigs (or ingots) of lead. In the wake of the military came civilian settlement. Small farmsteads were established at The Burrs, Chelmorton, at Chee Tor above Millers Dale with its impressive terraced fields, and at Roystone Grange, Ballidon, where extensive remains of a native Roman farmstead and its associated field systems can be seen. Buxton was established, as the spa-town of *Aquae Armenetia*, but the only other substantial civilian settlements were those that built up around the Roman forts, to meet the various needs of the troops stationed there.

With the removal of the Roman legions at the beginning of the 5th century, the Peak District sank into the relative obscurity of the Dark Ages. Little is known of the people of the Peak until the late 7th century, when the 'Tribal Hidage', drawn up to assess the taxable value of the kingdom of Mercia and its dependents, has a reference to the Pecsaetan, 'the dwellers of the Peak'. It is their remains that have been found in pagan burial places, in barrows such as Wigber Low and Benty Grange, complete with weapons of iron and ornaments of precious metals. Major events occurred in and around the area in the 9th and 10th centuries AD, but there is little physical evidence to record the Anglo-Saxon conquest of Anglian Mercia in 827, the Viking raids (which culminated in their annexation of Mercia in 874 and the founding of Derby), or the reconquest of the region by Edward the Elder in 920. In that year Edward built a fortress at Bakewell, where he received the submission of various northern leaders. Isolated monuments like the Grey Ditch at Bradwell, a bank and ditch closing off a valley route south into Mercia, may date from this period, reflecting the one-time border between Mercia and its northern neighbour Northumbria.

Stone crosses
One outstanding survival from the period is the numerous fragments of decorated stonework, particularly crosses. Thought to be mainly early Christian preaching crosses, used before churches were built, examples can be found in the churchyards of Hope, Eyam, Bakewell and Bradbourne. Highly-decorated tombstone slabs can also be found at Wirksworth and at Bakewell.

Norman castles
Twenty years after the Norman Conquest, William ordered a survey of his kingdom, the results of which were recorded in *Domesday*. Many Peakland villages were included, suggesting that occupation of the Peak was quite extensive by the 11th century AD. One of the lasting monuments to the Conquest is the gaunt ruin of Peveril Castle overlooking Castleton. It was given initially to William Peveril, the Conqueror's illegitimate son, and Castleton was developed as a planned town at its foot, though it never prospered. The castle also served as a hunting lodge for forays out into the Royal Forest of the Peak, which covered some 40 square miles of surrounding country. An example of the more usual motte and bailey castle can be seen at Pilsbury, near Hartington.

The Middle Ages
The 12th and 13th centuries were generally a time of expansion in medieval England. But a series of bad harvests and the Black Death in the mid-14th century wiped out up to a third of the population,

Against this superb Saxon cross the fine old church at Eyam is a brash newcomer

Perhaps the most enduring of man's works in the Peak are the narrow fields with which he striped the hills

and many villages were either deserted or deliberately depopulated, as landlords converted their lands to sheep and wool production.

Sheep featured large in the economy of the Peak in the 12th to the 14th centuries, when monastic houses outside the area established sheep granges on the verdant grassland of the White Peak. Virtually every modern farm with 'grange' in its name originated in this way, having originally been worked by lay brethren and local labour.

Those villages which were left after the 14th-century recession prospered. In Tideswell the magnificant Perpendicular parish church, known as the 'Cathedral of the Peak', was built almost completely in the 14th century from the profits of wool and lead. In many areas the undulating 'ridge and furrow' of medieval fields can still be seen. Some of the finest examples occur around Bradbourne, Fenny Bentley and Tissington, and in the Lower Manifold Valley around Throwley, where particularly extensive terraces of lynchets have survived, a means of creating level ground from the hillslopes.

Enclosures
In many ways the present-day character of the Peak District landscapes began to develop in the 17th and 18th centuries. This was the period when many of the limestone and gritstone farmhouses, each with their attendant cluster of farm buildings, were built. Medieval open fields were enclosed by agreement and stone walls were built, preserving the characteristic reversed S-shape of medieval ridge and furrow fields. These, seen around villages such as Chelmorton, Litton, Tideswell and Flagg, are an essential part of the Peakland landscape. They gave rise to Celia Fiennes' comment (in her *Journeys*) that '. . . you see neither hedge nor tree but only low drye stone walls round some ground. . . .' At the time she was writing, in about 1700, much of

Hikers resting their packs at a stone packhorse bridge, by which an ancient equestrian trading route crosses the tumbling River Goyt

Bridge building in the Peak reached its height when Monsal Dale was spanned by this majestic viaduct

the Peak District was unenclosed. A century later, with the Enclosure Movement in full swing, enormous areas were being divided into the geometric field patterns that can be seen today. Hundreds of miles of stone walls were constructed as heath and common grazing land were enclosed and spread with tons of locally-produced lime to encourage the growth of sweet Peakland grass for cattle and sheep.

Road and rail

The Peak was slow to lose its remoteness. Many pack-horse routes, still visible on the moors east of the Derwent, crossed the Peak in the medieval period and were used by long trains of animals carrying salt and cheese from Cheshire and the west, returning with lime, lead and stone. Pack-horse bridges, narrow with low parapets to avoid the panniers, survive at Edale and elsewhere. Good roads though were sadly lacking. Indeed, Celia Fiennes, in her journey through Derbyshire, asserted '. . . you are forced to have Guides as in all parts of Derbyshire . . .' and '. . . the common people know not above 2 or 3 miles from their home. . . .' In the

second half of the 18th century, turnpike roads began to make their way through the area, providing for the first time a reasonable road-transport system along which agricultural and mineral produce could be moved more rapidly and cheaply. With no canals through the region, the roads carried considerable traffic until, in the 19th century, an alternative was offered by the railways. The Cromford and High Peak Railway was a direct competitor after its opening in 1831, particularly for bulky minerals.

Lead-mining

The Industrial Revolution made its mark even in the remote fastnesses of the Peak in the 18th and 19th centuries. Lead production, important for centuries but worked only on a relatively small scale, increased rapidly with advances in smelting technology. This led to a proliferation of mines and engine houses, furnaces and condensers, and large tracts of ravaged countryside bear testimony to the industrial exploitation. Limestone quarrying, initially on a small scale to provide for local needs, also expanded, both as a result of the increased local agricultural demand for lime and with the increased ability of the companies to move the finished product out of the Peak District. Gritstone quarrying flourished, for building materials and for grindstones and millstones, large numbers of which can still be found abandoned in quarries that no longer ring to the sound of the mason's hammer.

The Peak District landscapes have always proved attractive to man. The rugged gritstone moors have provided hunting and pasture, while the more mellow limestone has offered plentiful grazing and the opportunity to grow crops in sheltered locations. Both have provided enormous quantities of minerals over the centuries, to supply and sustain developing agriculture and industry. The signs of this human impact on the landscapes are everywhere, waiting to be appreciated.

The Story of a National Park

During the 1930s life in the great industrial cities which flank the southern Pennines was grim. The country was in the depths of the Depression, unemployment was soaring, and the post Great War promise of 'a land fit for heroes' had a hollow, empty ring. The teeming populations of Manchester, Sheffield, Stoke-on-Trent and Derby found little to cheer them in the pervading gloom. But there was one escape route from their back-to-back terraces. Beyond the smoky streets the blue, misty outline of the moors beckoned. The Peak District had long been an important 'lung' for the recreation of city dwellers, who flooded out at weekends and holidays by bus and train in huge numbers.

Recording this phenomenon in *The Untutored Townsman's Invasion of the Country*, Professor Cyril Joad wrote: 'In our day, hiking has replaced beer as the shortest cut out of Manchester, as turning their backs upon the cities which their fathers made, armies of young people make sorties at any and every opportunity into the countryside.' Patrick Monkhouse, in *On Foot in the Peak* published in 1932, confirmed: 'The movement which has brought young townsfolk out on to the moors has hardly a parallel elsewhere in Britain. For an hour on Sunday mornings it looks like Bank Holiday in the Manchester stations, except that families do not go to Blackpool for Whit-week in shorts. Southcountrymen gasp to look at it.'

Forbidden ground

However, as Professor Joad recounted, on all this country there was laid 'the curse of the keeper'. Vast areas of the highest, most spectacular moors of the Peak District were strictly preserved for the rearing, management and shooting of red grouse, or as water-gathering grounds by the municipal authorities. Stern-faced gamekeepers were

employed to keep the ramblers off the moors of Kinder Scout, Bleaklow and the eastern moors. The moorland edges were dotted with 'Trespassers will be Prosecuted' signs, which the ramblers called 'wooden liars' because they had no power in law. Straying off one of the few footpaths could result in an encounter with a keeper not averse to bully-boy eviction tactics.

Walking guides of the day actually warned ramblers where to watch out for unfriendly gamekeepers. Monkhouse, describing a short cut from South Head to Edale Cross on Kinder in *On Foot in the Peak* said a gamekeeper could be seen 'on populous Sundays' sitting with a dog and a gun on the side of South Head. 'His presence is usually an adequate deterrent, and the gun has not yet been used.' The classic walkers guide, *Across the Derbyshire Moors* by John Derry, warned in 1926, 'Nothing keeps alive the spirit of revolt and iconoclasm so fiercely as a refusal to the general community of the use of their eyes over beautiful remote tracts of the earth, under the plea of private ownership.' The owners were determined to keep the ramblers off, and some even went to the length of publishing photographs of walkers on Kinder Scout in local newspapers, with a reward for their identification. More liberal landowners issued permits for walkers.

Gaining access

Pressure for access to these high and lonely places grew through the 1920s and 1930s in the wake of unemployment and the new political awareness of the working class. Protest rallies, some attended by up to 10,000 ramblers, were held in the Winnats Pass and Cave Dale, near Castleton. They called for free access to mountain and moorland, and significantly, for the creation of National Parks. Eventually and inevitably, the issue came to a head with the celebrated Mass Trespass on to Kinder Scout on 24 April 1932. About 400 ramblers set out from Hayfield with the well-publicised intention of trespassing on the forbidden moorland of Kinder. As they left the confines of William Clough and approached the plateau edge below Sandy Heys, they encountered groups of keepers, and scuffles broke out. As a result, six ramblers were arrested, charged with riotous assembly and assault, and five received prison sentences of between two and six months at Derby Assizes.

Kinder Scout, where only privileged feet trod before 400 walkers defied owners in a battle for free access to the moors. Their protests helped make possible today's National Park, whose millstone symbol recalls both local grit and an old Peakland industry

Many people have since questioned the need for, and effectiveness of, the Mass Trespass, which was followed by others that received much less publicity. But there can be no doubt that it proved to be one of the most important catalysts for the National Parks and access to the countryside legislation which followed World War II. In his report on National Parks to the post-war Labour government, Sir Arthur Hobhouse pointed out: 'The controversy over access to uncultivated lands reaches its height in the Peak, where landowners may draw their most remunerative rents from the lease of grouse moors, and where at the same time large areas are sterilised for water catchment. Many of the finest moorlands, where thousands wish to wander, are closed against 'trespassers' and an altercation with a gamekeeper may often mar a day's serenity. A National Park in the Peak District will not justify its name unless this problem is satisfactorily solved.'

Upper Derwent, where reservoirs and afforestation have softened a stern landscape and added extra dimensions to a naturally varied countryside

Access was not the only reason why the Peak became the first British National Park.

Within two years of its inception in 1951, the first agreement allowing free access, except for a few days during the grouse-shooting season, had been signed. Today, 76 square miles of the northern and eastern moors, including the infamous 'battlegrounds' of the 1930s, are subject to agreements between the National Park and landowners. Access land in the Peak still accounts for 60 per cent of the total in the country.

Hobhouse had reported: '. . . beyond its intrinsic qualities, the Peak has a unique value as a National Park, surrounded as it is on all sides by industrial towns and cities. Sheffield, Manchester, Huddersfield, Derby and The Potteries lie on its borders; indeed, it is estimated that half the population of England lives within 60 miles of Buxton. There is no other area which has evoked more strenuous public effort to safeguard its beauty

. . . Its very proximity to the industrial towns renders it as vulnerable as it is valuable.' Those threats included mineral extraction, regarded by Hobhouse as the most serious menace and still the greatest threat to the National Park today; the flooding of valleys for reservoirs; afforestation by alien conifers; and the insidious spread of suburbs.

What is a National Park?

There are still many misconceptions about our National Parks. Unlike those of the USA and most other countries, British National Parks are not owned by the nation. The majority of land in them is in private hands, their being the home and workplace of local people. The usually-accepted definition is that first coined by architect and planner John Dower, in his seminal 1945 report which laid down the blueprint for our Parks. A National Park is:

'An extensive area of beautiful and relatively wild country in which, for the nation's benefit and by appropriate national decision and action,
   (a) the characteristic landscape beauty is strictly preserved,
   (b) access and facilities for public open-air enjoyment are amply provided,
   (c) wildlife and buildings and places of architectural and historic interest are suitably protected while
   (d) established farming use is effectively maintained.'

The National Park is administered by a local-government authority known as the Peak Park Joint Planning Board. This body takes on the planning powers of the six county councils in whose area it lies, and also provides facilities and services for the estimated 20 million visitors it receives every year. Two-thirds of the governing Board represent local county and district councils, while the remaining is appointed by the Government to look after national interests (although most members are also local people). Approximately 75 per cent of its income comes from central-government grant support, and the rest from local rates.

Schemes and services

One of the other benefits which came from access agreements was the creation of the Park's highly-respected Ranger Service (see page 27), which acts as the essential link between locals and visitors.

Another vital link between the visiting public (most of whom still come from the surrounding cities), and the National Park is the Information Service, which runs eight centres throughout the Park and produces a wide range of publications, walks and talks. Here the second duty of providing facilities for public enjoyment is met, and the Park's residential-study centre at Losehill Hall in Castleton caters for those who wish to learn more about this landscape.

Nevertheless the National Park's first duty is as a planning authority, and it has exercised its planning role in several innovative ways designed to benefit both visitor and local alike. An example of this was the Goyt Valley Traffic Scheme, which closed off a popular valley to traffic at busy times and provided alternatives, a system since copied in the Upper Derwent Valley.

Right: many of the small, informal walled fields in the Peak date from before the 18th-century Enclosures, and a few are of Celtic origin

Bridges, embankments and cuttings add interest to long and evenly-graded trails that have been established for cyclists and walkers along old railway trackbeds throughout the National Park

Railway trails

When two railway lines crossing the White Peak plateau closed within a few weeks of each other in the late 1960s, the Peak Board stepped in to create the popular Tissington and High Peak Trails, thus preserving them and providing walkers, riders and cyclists with routes across some of the Park's finest scenery. Bicycles can be hired on the Tissington Trail (the former Ashbourne to Buxton route), and on the High Peak Trail (once the Cromford and High Peak line). The authority has since also bought the former Midland line to create the Monsal Trail along the Wye Valley. John Ruskin protested at the building of the Monsal Viaduct across the Wye; today it is one of the railway structures which have been considered well worth preserving in the conversion of the old routes.

Stone tents

A number of farm barns have also been converted – into 'stone tents' or 'camping barns', offering simple overnight accommodation for a small fee. They offer a space to sleep, a place to wash, a cooking area (but no cooking equipment), and shelter. As well as providing a roof for walkers and cyclists, they also make use of buildings which have become redundant for farm use but still contribute a good deal to the landscape.

Integration

The 'Routes for People' scheme in the White Peak area sought to separate the potentially dangerous mixture of heavy quarry traffic from holiday motorists in an integrated network of specialist routes, with picnic areas and waymarked walks.

The theme of integration has been expanded further in recent years to cover whole village communities in the 'Integrated Rural Development' programme (IRD) in Longnor and Monyash. A pooling of resources and a willingness to co-operate and compromise has led to an exciting departure in

The train has gone but the viaduct remains as a superb viewpoint from which Monsal Trail walkers can appreciate the beautiful Wye Valley

countryside planning and management. Farmers have been paid, not for harmful chemical sprays, but for the number of wild flowers in their hay meadows; not for alien post-and-wire fences, but for the maintenance of their traditional and attractive dry-stone walls.

Patrick Monkhouse wrote half a century ago that people had never been more conscious of the beauty of hills and dales, and never thought it more important that beauty should remain beautiful. Surely those sentiments still hold true.

Wildlife of the Peak

The Peak District – at the southern end of the Pennine Chain – contrasts markedly in scenery and wildlife with the lowlands which surround it. Within the National Park too are striking variations in scenery, caused by differences in the underlying rocks.

At the centre is the 'White Peak', a region of Carboniferous limestone measuring roughly 10 miles from the River Hamps in the west to the River Derwent in the east. Much of the region forms a plateau of some 1,000ft altitude, scored by a network of steep-sided dales cut by water erosion, but now often dry. Unlike the plateau itself, they are rich reservoirs of wildlife.

Underground, as in all limestone regions, the dissolving action of rainwater has formed many channels and caverns. Some have become popular tourist attractions, while others can only be seen by the intrepid caver.

Surrounding the White Peak is a horseshoe of moorland known as the 'Dark Peak', a dramatic landscape formed by massive sandstone rocks known as millstone grit – from their usage in the past. This culminates in the dual plateaux of Kinder Scout and Bleaklow, both over 2,000ft.

A perfect example of Peakland habitats, with the craggy crest and grassy slopes of Chrome Hill overlooking riverside woodland and valley pasture alongside the River Dove

In the east of the Park is a series of gritstone escarpments or 'edges' – beloved by climbers – which face across the distant River Derwent towards the limestone. To the west the gritstone forms Axe Edge and The Roaches. Other rocks are seen strikingly exposed in a huge landslip at Mam Tor, near Castleton.

Moorlands of the Dark Peak

Perhaps the most conspicuous feature of the Dark Peak is its heather, which is managed by spring burning to encourage tender new shoots and

Where the going is tough, only the tough survive – like the moorland heathers (top) and cotton grass (upper right). But in their shelter can be found more tender types, like the bog asphodel (right)

enables the ground to support sheep and grouse. In wetter areas the vegetation is dominated by hare's-tail cottongrass, which when fruiting makes the ground look as if it is covered with cotton wool. Drier moorland supports black-fruited bilberry, red-fruited cowberry and the crowberry.

More localised is the cloudberry, a northern species whose raspberry-like leaves and white flowers are seen around Kinder Scout and Bleaklow. Its orange fruit is now rarely found – perhaps because of increased sheep grazing – but last century was harvested for local markets.

The peat on the upper moors is badly eroded – as is obvious to anyone driving over the A57 Snake Pass between Sheffield and Glossop, and even more so to Pennine Way walkers struggling through the loose, sticky masses that cover the surface. Some of the damage may have been caused by widespread fires in recent drought years, or overgrazing by sheep.

On steep slopes below the peat level is rough

grassland which commonly includes tussocky mat-grass tough enough to resist even sheep – but all too often such areas have become poisonous seas of bracken.

Springs and seepáge zones are marked by patches of soft rush and often carpeted with *Sphagnum* bog moss, occasionally sharing the damp habitat with bog asphodel and the insectivorous sundew.

Hidden inhabitants

At first glance the casual visitor may find the moors bleak, but they have a rich variety of insects and other small animals. Most conspicuous are some of the larger moths and their larvae, including the large, hairy, black-and-brown caterpillars of the northern oak eggar, which are often found amongst the heather. The adult has an impressive wingspan of up to 4in. In either form it is easily distinguished from the Emperor moth, which has obvious 'eye' markings on its wings and produces green and black caterpillars.

Butterflies are relatively few. The most characteristic is the green hairstreak, which is often found on flowering bilberry in the late spring.

Moorland birds and their distinctive calls lend a special character to the uplands. The most common breeding species is the meadow pipit, but also found are skylarks and – less commonly – curlews, golden plovers and merlin. Bright colouring and the metallic clatter of its call makes the red grouse one

The Emperor moth's larvae feed on heather

The pastoral White Peak

Views of the White Peak from the A623 road north of Tideswell encompass a panorama of rolling green fields cut by white limestone walls – typical of the plateau and in direct contrast to the country of the Dark Peak. Yet fewer than 200 years ago most of this was covered with heather, and it was only when the open land was enclosed that it began to take on its present, softer complexion. Remnants of White Peak heath survive on the highest ground above Bradwell and Great Longstone, and can also be seen beside the

The lime-loving meadow cranesbill is one of several native geraniums found beside White Peak lanes

of the most obvious species, fairly easily seen as it feeds on the young heather shoots that are its staple diet. Not so obvious are its chicks, whose camouflage blends perfectly with the old heather in which the birds nest.

Of the few mammals that live on the upland, perhaps the most distinctive is the mountain hare. This was re-introduced to Derbyshire during the 19th century and has become well established on Kinder Scout and the eastern moors. In winter it turns completely white.

Peak woodlands

Peak District woodlands survive in a few of the valleys, or 'cloughs', and on the gritstone are dominated by sessile oak with scattered birch – plus rowan and alder alongside streams. Good examples include Padley Wood, which is near Sheffield on the National Trust's Longshaw Estate, as well as Ladybower and Priddock Woods – which overlook Ladybower Reservoir and are both managed by the Derbyshire Wildlife Trust as nature reserves.

Between the trees the ground cover is mainly bilberry and wavy-hair grass, interspersed with several types of fern, and only near streams can there be found more varied flora. Large ant heaps are inhabited by the hairy-eyed wood ant, whose soldiers defend the colony from intruders by spraying formic acid. The oaks themselves are home to many creatures, and in spring support massive hatches of moth caterpillars, a major source of food for blue tits, coal tits and great tits, warblers, redstarts and – encouraged to breed at the limit of their range by nestboxes – pied flycatchers. Other larvae are extracted from the timber by woodpeckers, and the green woodpecker is attracted by wood ants.

Sadly, these interesting remnants of native woodlands and the fine opportunities for natural-history study they present are far outstripped by conifer plantations, which support few ground plants but are of interest as strongholds for the red squirrel and nesting sites for sparrowhawks.

A515 road south of Newhaven.

A few colourful hay meadows survive from the past, and many wild plants are found along the wide roadside verges. In summer the older fields may be yellow with buttercups, while cow parsley and hogweed fringe the lanes with white flowers before making way for the blue of meadow cranesbill – known locally as 'thunderclouds' because it blooms in the July period of thunderstorms.

Strikingly different flora is found in grassland which has colonised along the lines of lead veins or 'rakes', and around their attendant workings. Mineral bands traversing the plateau rise to the surface of the limestone and often run for miles. Many have not been worked for centuries – or at worst, have been disturbed only intermittently – and not even farm animals present a threat, since they are usually prevented from grazing the lead-impregnated vegetation.

One of the most conspicuous plants associated with the rakes is the yellow mountain pansy, while in areas of loose debris during June or July can be found the white flowers of spring sandwort – also known as leadwort because of its habitat.

There are few birds on the White Peak plateau, because the ground-nesting species commonly associated with fields – lapwings, meadow pipits and skylarks, for instance – are unable to withstand the frequent disruption of grass cutting for silage.

Various animals have survived by taking refuge in the dry-stone walls of the field boundaries, including several species of vole and shrew, the stoats and weasels that prey on them, and nesting wheatears and stonechats.

The Dales

The Dales account for only a small proportion of the Peak National Park, but they are its most valuable wildlife resource.

Five of them are included in the Derbyshire

Dales National Nature Reserve – which is managed by the Nature Conservancy Council, Britain's official nature-conservation body. Other areas are protected by the Derbyshire Wildlife Trust and National Trust.

Before exploitation during and prior to the medieval period the dales were naturally wooded, probably with a variety of trees. Nowadays the commonest species in the natural woodlands are ash and elm, though this balance is changing due to the ravages of Dutch elm disease. Closer to villages there are woods planted specifically to provide a crop of timber. Some of these may be almost entirely of ash or sycamore.

Below the leaf canopy in the natural woods is a

Bloody cranesbill grows alongside the Peak Trails

Wheatears are often seen flitting along drystone walls and across the bare hillside scree

wide diversity of plants, including hazel, bird cherry, guelder rose and occasionally such rarities as mountain currant and the early-flowering mezereon. Spring brings colourful displays of bluebells, yellow archangel, sweet woodruff and – on damper soils – the white, clustered stars of the garlic-like ransoms.

Late spring is a good time for bird watching in dales woodland, when the chaffinch and willow warbler are found with the chiff-chaff, wood warbler, spotted flycatcher and both the great-spotted and green woodpecker.

Scrub, also common in the dales, has greatly increased since the rabbit population was reduced by myxomatosis in the 1950s. Hawthorn in particular has reduced interesting grassland to such an extent that much time and energy has been

given to its removal – especially from nature reserves. Other scrub areas – particularly those of hazel – are quite different in character and of much greater interest. Among their rare flora can be found lily of the valley, bloody cranesbill and globeflower.

Grassland slopes

Grassland in the dales is similarly rich in flowers during late spring, with the royal spikes of early-purple orchids and yellow of cowslips painting bright splashes of colour on the valley slopes. Later they are replaced by smaller summer plants – the gold of bird's-foot trefoil and common rock rose contrasting with purple thyme. The most visible of the many insects on the sunny, south-facing slopes are the butterflies, starting early in the season with the orange tip and green hairstreak, which give way to the common blue in summer. Also in this warm, dry habitat is one of the few reptiles to be found in the dales – the harmless slow worm, a snake-like legless lizard which shelters under stones and logs in hot weather.

These grassland areas depend for their continued existence on regular grazing by sheep or cattle, now much less prevalent than formerly.

On some of the steeper slopes – particularly below crags is seen the uncommon limestone fern, which is beautifully delicate in appearance but sufficiently tough to survive the arid conditions that can prevail. Excellent views of these isolated and often inaccessible 'reserves' can be enjoyed from the Monsal Trail, a walk which follows the course of the one-time Midland Railway.

Waterlife

Only a few of the valleys feature permanent rivers – in particular the Dove, Lathkill and Wye, all of which flow through a series of dales. Their trout fishing has been renowned for centuries. Indeed, during 1676 no less an angler than Charles Cotton wrote of the Lathkill in Izaak Walton's *The Compleat Angler*, '. . . it is, by many degrees the purest and most transparent stream that I ever yet saw, either at home or abroad; and breeds, 'tis said, the reddest and best Trouts in England.'

Little has changed. The Lathkill is still one of the country's purest rivers, still supports a wealth of aquatic life from the smallest larvae to the largest fish – and still provides immense pleasure.

River birds in the Peak District include the bright kingfisher, which is seen darting along the streams in search of small fish; the bobbing dipper, which walks underwater to find its prey; and both pied and grey wagtails, constantly engaged in hunting insects along limestone and gritstone banks. Competing with the wagtails are Daubenton's bats, which flit over the water at dusk.

In the northern part of the National Park are several water reservoirs – the best known being the Derwent Valley complex, of which Ladybower is the largest. None is particularly noted for large concentrations of water fowl, but they do provide breeding grounds for teal and winter quarters for pochard, goldeneye and goosander. Common sandpipers breed on the shores.

Unique in having such contrasting scenery and wildlife so close together, the Peak National Park's attractions depend on a fragile web of life that could easily be broken by abuse or thoughtlessness. Only a tiny fraction of the area can be protected as nature reserves, with the fate of the remainder in the hands of owners, farmers and visitors.

Lead Mining in the Peak

Extensive surface remains survive at Magpie Mine, Sheldon, including a 'Cornish' engine house of 1869. Below: a mine team photographed at the turn of the century. The man on the left has a bunch of tallow dips

Lead mining and agriculture were the principle industries in the White Peak from the time of the Roman occupation until the exhausted mines succumbed to cheap imports of foreign lead during the 1870s. The limestone rock is criss-crossed by countless mineral veins, the most common type being 'scrins' which formed where mineralising fluids filled vertical joints a few inches wide in the limestone. 'Rake' veins are similar but much wider, being mineralised faults, whereas 'pipe' veins were formed by the deposition of minerals in natural caverns. Scattered along the courses of these veins are some 30,000 abandoned lead-mine workings, yet these man-made scars have blended back into the landscape and are no longer obtrusive, their aura of mystery heightened by their curious names: Joseph's Dream, Hit or Miss, Hanging Eye, Boggart Hole, Trusty Friend, Wanton Legs, Nell I'll Tickle Thee.

Conditions underground were often cramped, wet and cold, the work being both dangerous and physically exhausting. The miners were of a rough, unhealthy appearance and they spoke a broad dialect, using many specialised mining terms which were unintelligible to visitors from other areas. Daniel Defoe, writing early in the 18th century, described a Wirksworth miner as 'a most uncouth spectacle . . . clothed all in leather . . . lean as a skeleton, pale as a dead corpse'. Women were not employed underground, but many found work 'dressing' ore.

Frequent accidents

Accidents were all too frequent, the worst resulting from explosions of firedamp (methane from the shale strata) such as at Mawstone Mine, Youlgreave, which left eight dead, including three members of a rescue party.

Right: the centre figure of this trio, Mr Fox, was entombed for three days in Townend Mine Left: small, carved figure of a female ore dresser. Below: bronze dish that was once the standard measure of ore in the Low Peak. It holds some 14 pints

kept there for the measurement of lead ore. It is made of bronze and dates to the reign of Henry VIII, and all the individual dishes belonging to the liberties had to match the contents of this one. Low Peak dishes are rectangular, while those of the High Peak resemble small wooden tubs.

Miners prospecting for veins of lead in the King's Field were authorised 'by the custom of the mine to dig, delve, search, subvert, and overturn all manner of grounds, lands, meadows, closes, pastures, mears and marshes, for ore mines of whose inheritance soever they be; dwelling-houses, orchards and gardens excepted'. Other exceptions included highways and churchyards. Various conditions were usually observed by a miner staking a claim, and after the barmaster and two jurymen had confirmed his 'title', he was able to proceed without seeking consent from the land-owner. He could also proceed without permission from anybody, under 'squatter's rights'. If, however, he failed to ratify his claim by producing lead, he was under obligation to redress any damage caused by his excavations. If successful, he was entitled to cut down timber required for his mining operations, and had access to the nearest highway and running water. The verbal laws were compounded into an Act of Parliament which became law in 1851 and 52.

Laws and customs

Many miners worked at their own small mines and had a ruggedly independent way of life, being literally a law unto themselves. A code of customs which governed every aspect of lead mining had developed gradually over the centuries and was first written down as early as 1288. In each 'liberty' (roughly equivalent to a township) these zealously defended customs were administered by courts consisting of elected miners, supervised by a steward and barmaster appointed by the Lords of the Mineral Field. The latter represented the interests of the Crown, which claimed many mineral rights and revenues. Tithe was paid to the Church. The tribunal of miners made and administered the unique laws by which the industry was governed, becoming virtually independent of all civil law, conducting inquests in the event of fatalities, and exercising the right to punish miners guilty of crimes against their fellows. The theft of ore was a very serious offence, and the first and second convictions were punished by fines of 3s 4d and 6s 8d respectively, but the law for a third conviction decreed that the guilty person had his right hand impaled to the winding structure at the shaft top.

The laws, customs, privileges and entitlements of the industry were listed in a *Rhymed Chronicle* composed by Edward Manlove, a Steward of the Low Peak Courts at Wirksworth, where the Grand Jury met in the Moot Hall. The Standard Dish is

Early history

North of Ballidon at Roystone Grange archaeological excavations have revealed a Roman wall constructed over an opencast lead vein working. The only other evidence of such early mining is the Roman pigs of lead found scattered about the country; inscriptions on these show that they came from *Lutudarum* (perhaps the Roman name for the Peak District) and did not contain silver. After the Roman occupation had ended, mining presumably continued on a smaller scale from opencast sites on the more prominent veins. In 1086 *Domesday* listed seven 'lead works' in

Derbyshire, although these were probably smelting sites. Odin Mine at Castleton is recorded as early as 1280, and by 1470 there was underground mining at the Nestus Mines, Matlock.

Driving the soughs

By 1600 some of the richest rake veins had already been worked out down to the natural water table. Effective pumping equipment was not available, so the answer was to dig drainage levels – locally called soughs (pronounced suffs). The first was made during 1632-51 by a Dutch drainage expert, Sir Cornelius Vermuyden, to drain Gang Mine at Cromford. Later soughs had to be progressively deeper and longer, lowering the water table throughout vast areas and making possible new eras of prosperity for the richest mining fields at Wirksworth, Winster, Alport and Eyam.

There were few aids to the work – the earliest documented use of gunpowder in British mining was at Bailey Croft Sough, Wirksworth, in 1672, but its danger and expense encouraged miners to persist with traditional techniques. Levels were driven through hard ground using a hammer and pick to cut a succession of sweeping parallel grooves in the 'forefield' (or tunnel face), which was advanced only about two inches per shift.

A sequence of soughs was driven into each productive mineral field – at Gang Mine, the Dutchman's Level was soon made redundant by the slightly deeper Bates Sough, which was in turn superseded by Cromford Sough. Begun in about 1672, Cromford Sough eventually attained a length of three miles by 1800. The outflow from Cromford Sough helped to power Arkwright's cotton mill until most of its water was taken by the even deeper Meerbrook Sough which was started in 1772 and by 1806 had already cost £43,745.

There were once over 100 steam engines in Peak District mines, some used for winding and ore-crushing rather than pumping. But their success was limited since coal was so expensive and few lead mines could afford the running costs. In contrast the enormous cost of a major sough was underwritten by wealthy speculators who hoped to recoup their outlay by receiving a proportion of the ore obtained from the numerous mines thereby relieved.

This drainage sough is easily accessible beside the path in Lathkill Dale, and dates from around 1800

Mill Close, Britain's largest lead mine, had produced 430,000 tons of ore by 1938, when it flooded out

Water pressure engines (powered by water falling down the mine shaft and flowing out along a sough) and waterwheels both used a cheap source of power, but often proved impractical in the Peak District, where surface water supplies tend to fail during the summer. A waterwheel installed at Lathkill Dale Mine in 1836 was 52ft in diameter, and at the adjacent Mandale Mine a 35ft diameter wheel was supplied by an aqueduct, the columns of which still cross that picturesque valley.

Riches or ruin

Lead mining was always a financial gamble because of the unpredictability of the veins, which could suddenly 'pinch' out to nothing or 'belly' into a rich pipe. The latter occurred at Ball Eye Mine, Bonsall, where the miners found a 'mass of lead' 50ft high and 120ft wide, worth £12,000. Veins were frequently cut off by lava flows or faults: at Hucklow the High Rake Mining Company lost over £19,000 sinking a shaft 720ft through volcanic rock without meeting the hoped-for limestone strata. Sometimes natural caverns were met and one found at Ball Eye Mine before 1661 contained a mammoth's skull – which greatly puzzled the miners. The workings of adjacent mines frequently intersected underground, and the ensuing legal disputes nearly drove the shareholders to despair. In 1833, after the Magpie workings had broken into Great Redsoil Mine at Sheldon, both sides lit sulphurous fires underground to smoke out their opponents. Three miners died.

By the 19th century veins were becoming exhausted and the odds were stacked against mining speculations. However, a few large ore strikes still occurred, and the legendary Gang Mine made a profit of £8,067 in 1813. The more usual story was of decline: Gregory Mine at Ashover – which had yielded £15,024 profit during 1772 – closed in 1803 after a series of large losses and the nearby Overton Mine suffered a similar fate.

Speculation reached fever pitch during the 1850s after it became possible to form limited liability companies. Many very dubious enterprises were launched and the gullible shareholders fleeced: there was even a project to mine gold in Lathkill Dale – nothing seemed impossible. Eventually the investors became wary and, as a result of a drastic fall in the price of lead ore, nearly all mines were

Visitors to Peak Cavern, at Castleton, can explore a curious underground canal by boat

abandoned before 1900. Mill Close Mine at Darley Dale survived this general decline, having been re-opened in 1859 by Edward Miller Wass, who installed efficient steam engines and struck a vast quantity of ore. By the time Mill Close was flooded out in 1938, it had produced 430,000 tons.

The last attempt to mine lead in Derbyshire was in 1952. Some 200,000 tons of fluorspar are mined annually near Eyam, yielding 4,000 tons of lead ore. Calcite is extracted from Long Rake near Youlgreave, and limestone at Middleton-by-Wirksworth! Along the western flank of the Peak District there are several abandoned copper mines, those at Ecton in the Manifold Valley having yielded a profit of £335,000 during 1760-1817. In addition, silver, zinc, iron and manganese ores, coal, chert, black marble and Blue John were all once part of the rich harvest.

The legacy

Two thousand years of lead mining have left the Peak District riddled with shafts, now mostly collapsed, or capped for safety, although caution is still required when walking in the former mining areas. The courses of scrins and rakes are often delineated by rows of grass-covered hillocks with shafts or collapsed hollows every few yards and ruins of the miners' stone sheds ('coes'). Owing to the restrictive effect of the local mining customs and the poorness of the veins, a typical mine was remarkably small, its two or three owners working part-time and getting only about 10 tons of ore a year. Larger mines had engine shafts and winding gear operated by horses working gins.

Opencast lead workings on rakes resemble small gorges (Dirtlow Rake at Castleton is a fine example), but some sites have been devastated when reworked for fluorspar. Many interesting mineral specimens can be found on wasteheaps. The principal lead ore, galena (lead sulphide), is easily distinguished by its high density and silvery metallic lustre when freshly broken.

The chimneys and flues of old lead smelting furnaces can be seen at Meerbrook (near Alderwasley), Stone Edge (at Ashover), Bradwell and Alport. Often the most problematical remains at smelting sites are the lead particles which still permeate the vegetation and can poison livestock.

Abandoned mine workings are usually very unsafe and should never be explored by casual sightseers. Those curious about the underground world will find the Peak's show caves well worth a visit. At Castleton visitors to Speedwell Cavern are taken in a boat along a canal-like level which was driven during the 1770s in an attempt to locate a lead vein. The nearby Blue John and Treak Cliff caves yield a rare ornamental variety of fluorspar called Blue John; whereas Peak Cavern is an impressive natural cave – as is Poole's Cavern at Buxton. Bagshawe Cavern at Bradwell is a natural cave which was discovered when working Mulespinner Mine. Magpie Mine, Sheldon has more surface remains than any other mine in the Peak, and it is now a field study centre run by the Peak District Mines Historical Society. Visitors can see a Cornish engine house dating from 1869 and other extensive surface remains; the main shaft here is 728ft deep and its sough 'tail' (outlet) is conspicuous by the River Wye in Shacklow Wood, Ashford. There is a display of old lead mining equipment at the Tramway Museum, Crich.

Goodluck Mine (in the Via Gellia near Middleton-by-Wirksworth) was driven 150 years ago as a haulage level to serve some productive scrins; it gives visitors the most accurate impression of typical conditions experienced by the ancient miners. At Matlock Bath, the Great Rutland and Masson caverns reveal how Nestus Pipe was exploited during the 1670s, and on High Tor the Fern and Roman caves are opencast rake workings of great antiquity. Royal Cave and Temple Mine are both fluorspar workings dating only from the 1950s, but the former also contains remnants of Speedwell Lead Mine which was itself a show cave by the 1820s. Temple Mine has a display of mining equipment and is associated with the adjacent Peak District Lead Mining Museum at Matlock Bath. The principal exhibit here is a large water-pressure engine dating from 1819.

Peakland Customs

'Today the Peaklanders are as fond of dancing as ever, and although no piper produces eerie music at feast times they can still make a pretty show. The hill country has endowed the youths and maidens with suppleness and they trip it with exceeding grace. . . . Old customs are tenaciously preserved . . . in some places the wells are dressed for the festival of the patron saint. . . .
(Robert Murray Gilchrist)

Flowers often figure prominently in the folklore of rural areas where customs have lingered from one generation to another. This is particularly true of the custom of dressing wells as an appreciation of the gift of water, an observance largely confined to the Peak District. It is thought to have originated from the culture of Mediterranean countries where water was valued for cleansing, healing and refreshment, and may have been introduced during the Roman occupation of Britain. Wells found to have healing virtues were dedicated to nymphs

Wells dressing at its best. This fine example of floral artistry was created in the village of Hope, Derbyshire

Many hours of hard work go into wells dressing, for results that are exquisite but purely ephemeral

Flowers figure large in many folk traditions, as demonstrated by the headgear of this morris dancer

believed to preside over the waters, as in the instance of *Aquis Armenetia* at Buxton. Christian missionaries weaned their converts from this form of pagan worship of the wells by agreeing that they should be dedicated to saints of the early Church, and so the strewing of flowers to celebrate the festivals of *Floralia* or *Fontinalia* lapsed.

The custom was revived during the early 17th century at Tissington when a certain Mary Twigg is claimed to have resurrected it by hanging festoons of flowers over the village wells in thanksgiving for the population's immunity – attributed to an unfailing supply of pure water – to bubonic plague or drought. This simple gesture was followed later by the creation of geometrical patterns of flowers, ferns, lichens, mosses and other foliage pressed into a background of moist clay.

Boards, which form the basis of the frames, are pierced with holes and studded with nails to key the clay, then placed on trestles or bales of straw to facilitate the work of 'petalling'. Designs drawn on paper are placed on the clay, and the outlines traced through with knitting needles and other improvised tools. This work completed, the paper patterns are placed conveniently for reference. The outlines are then piped with seeds, rice and alder cones, and filled in with more durable vegetable materials such as leaves and lichens. Finally, the delicate work of petalling is carried out. The petals are inserted from the bottom of the picture like tiles on a roof, so that the paler parts are covered by the next and succeeding layers. This also allows rain or moisture to drain off.

Other villages adopted the idea, sometimes after an improved water supply had been introduced – as at Buxton, Wirksworth and Youlgreave. Over the years more have been added to the list. Victorian writers, such as Robert Murray Gilchrist and Joseph Hatton, give the impression that some of the results were crude both in design and execution, but this cannot be imputed to the present generation of floral tableaux. Techniques vary in some villages but the annual displays are of a very high standard and have become major tourist attractions.

Annual wakes

Wells dressing became integrated into the annual Wake, or patronal festival of a village, which celebrated the church's birthday. On Wake-eve a midnight vigil was held in the church to welcome its saint's day, and the following day was a holiday with morris dancing, sports and other entertainments. It was a time of family re-union, when daughters in domestic service and sons apprenticed to trade or agriculture returned to the parental home for a well-deserved holiday. Derbyshire's most popular folk song, *Hayfield Fair*, recalls how the dancers 'played for ale and cakes'. Unfermented ale was the common beverage before tea became cheap and popular, while the Wakes' cake was baked especially for the occasion.

Castleton garlanding

The Victorian novelist R M Gilchrist wrote: '. . . in one of the most remote villages (Castleton) every Oak Apple Day a quaint and pretty pageant enlivens the irregular grey streets'. He further comments that 'gaily dressed children dance what survives of the Morris . . . whilst King Charles and his lady wife . . . ride in state through the quaint streets. His majesty, in cavalier costume, has the upper part of his body covered with a gorgeous bouquet, in shape not unlike a beehive.'

There have been changes to the pattern over the years, for the royal couple were formerly attended by mounted courtiers dressed in Stuart costume, and preceded by a court jester sweeping the road with a besom but making sudden forays into the ranks of the spectators who were treated to acts of buffoonery. Since 1955, the role of the consort has been filled by a female.

The garland is on a crinoline-like frame of hoops decorated with oak leaves laced with garden and meadow flowers, and surmounted by a posy of flowers called the 'queen'. The six village inns take turns to make the garland, which – at the close of the ceremony – is hauled up the church tower and left to be dismantled by the weather. The 'queen' is placed on the nearby war memorial.

The reason the church tower figures is that until 1897 this was how the parishioners showed their appreciation of the bellringers – who also received their annual remuneration from a public collection

Old age and a Christian veneer do little to disguise an ancient significance in Castelton's Garland Day

Personal and poignant reminders in Ilam village church of young girls who died before their time

that was made on the same day.

Kit dressing

Another custom featuring garlands, now no longer observed, was that of Kit Dressing. This was carried out on 1 May when milk-maids decorated their wooden pails (kits) with garlands and trinkets and carried them on their heads in procession. Stephen Glover, the Derbyshire historian, stated that this custom was observed at Baslow during the annual Wakes: 'At Baslow, the rural festival of kit-dressing took place on the 4th of August, and in the present year (1829) was attended by the Baslow Band . . . There were a great number of persons from the surrounding country, and even more distant places, assembled to witness this rural fête.

Funeral garlands

Garlands usually remind us of revelry and rejoicing, but the faded examples preserved in St Giles's Church at Matlock, and those at Ashford-in-the-Water, Ilam and Trusley, are funeral garlands or 'virgin crants', referred to by Shakespeare in relation to the death of Ophelia.

They were bell-like frames of wood decorated with rosettes, ribbons and streamers, and enclosing a personal relic of the deceased girls in whose memory they had been made.

On the occasion of the funeral the garland was carried by friends of the dead girl, and after the service of committal suspended from the rafters of the church above the pew which she had usually occupied. Such garlands were in many churches until congregations complained that they were

gathering dust and cobwebs, and even reducing the light. Many churches followed the example of Hope, where in 1749 the churchwardens authorised the payment of 1s. 6d, 'for removing ye garlands to make ye church lighter'.

Funeral clubs

Village societies were established in many rural communities to avoid the indignity of pay-burying and pauper funerals. At pay-buryings the 'bidder' invited friends and neighbours to a funeral, but warned them that they were expected to make some financial contribution. Widows would sit in the doorway to welcome mourners who expressed their condolences and placed their coins in her outstretched apron, or in a basin. By the payment of weekly premiums of one penny or half-penny, the burial societies provided a scale of benefits governed by length of membership and age at death. It was thought that the introduction of the NHS would cancel out the need for funeral clubs, but some have survived to provide generous benefits which keep ahead of inflation.

Cow clubs were a form of insurance against injury or disease of cattle. Premiums were paid on each cow accepted into the society, of which two

Love Feasts, based on meetings of the early Church, originate from 18th-century religious revivalism

members were appointed to assess the value of the animals. Veterinary treatment was also available. Tideswell Cow Club still survives and supplies its members with official badges of membership.

Love feasts

The 18th-century religious revival, spearheaded by the Wesley brothers, converted multitudes of workers employed in mines and mills, farms and factories, and from every stratum of society to a pattern of religious life and worship which inspired them to build 'wayside Bethels' in remote hamlets, villages and industrial centres throughout the country. Like their founders, the preachers continued the principle of field-preaching by organising and conducting camp-meetings and covenant services. These incorporated 'love feasts', based on the meetings of the early Church and associated with the Last Supper. Such gatherings included a communion service in which the elements consisted of bread and water.

The Woodlands love-feast is held annually in a barn at Alport Castles Farm, near the Snake Pass, on the morning of the first Sunday in July.

Rush bearing

This was once a common custom in the Peak

Once a good way to get the church floor recovered, rush bearing has always been associated with celebration and today allows artistic scope too

District, but only Macclesfield Forest Church has retained the ceremony, observed on the nearest Sunday to 12 August. In his *Survey of Derbyshire* (1815), Farey wrote: 'An ancient custom still prevails in Chapel-en-le-Frith, Glossop, Hayfield, Mellor, Peak Forest, and other places in the north of the county, I believe, of keeping the floor of the church and pews therein, constantly strewed or littered with dried rushes; the process of renewing which annually is called the Rush-bearing, and is usually accompanied by much ceremony. The Rush-bearing in Peak Forest is held on Midsummer Eve in each year. In Chapel-en-le-Frith . . . in the latter end of August, on public notice from the churchwardens, of the rushes being mown and properly dried, in some marshy parts of the parish, where the young people assemble, and having loaded the rushes on carts, decorate the same with flowers and ribbons, and attend them to church in procession . . .' Hayfield Churchwarden Accounts have the entries:

1722. For rushes for church 2s 6d
1766. Upon the account of the Rush Cart 5s 0d

At Whitwell, hay mown in the Church Meadows was used, while straw sufficed at Scarcliffe because of the scarcity of rushes.

Clypping the church

This parochial festival has also gradually waned in popularity and is now continued only at Wirksworth and Burbage, near Buxton. 'Clypping' means clasping or embracing the parent church of a parish, when members of daughter churches join with the main congregation for a service. Some churches marked the occasion on Mothering Sunday. At Wirksworth, a procession led by the town band assembles at the market-place, and upon reaching the church continues to make a circuit of the building. The vicar, choristers and congregation clasp hands to form a human chain around the building as they sing. It is held on 8 September, or the nearest Sunday to that date.

At Burbage, near Buxton, a procession commences on the last Sunday in July at the Burbage Institute and marches to the music of a band. Parents and children encircle the church.

Beating the bounds

Hathersage has its 'gospel stone' built into the foundations of a wayside wall. It was one of the sites visited at Rogationtide by clergy, choir and congregation to seek God's blessing on the growing crops and vegetables, and ask His protection from famine, pestilence and other possible adversities. The prefix 'gospel' was variously attached to a tree at Ashover; a lead-mine near Calver; a well at Hayfield; tumulii at Flagg; a brow at Chapel-en-le-Frith; and heaps of stone near Eyam. In his poem 'Hesperides', Herrick has an allusion to this springtime custom:

'Dearest, bury me
Under that Holy-Oke, or Gospel Tree,
Where (though thou see'st not) thou may'st think upon
Me, when thou yearly go'st procession.'

The religious ceremony appears to have been combined with the civil custom of 'beating the bounds', when children accompanied their parents along the hedges, walls, lanes and streams which surrounded a parish. At strategic points the children were gently struck with canes, so that when they achieved parenthood they would remember the boundaries and be able to inform their own offspring. The reason for this custom was the illiteracy of most residents, to whom maps and written instructions had little meaning.

Padley Chapel pilgrimage

Padley Chapel is a surviving fragment of the ruined mansion of the family of Padley, later occupied by the Eyres and Fitzherberts. The two latter families were long renowned for their allegiance to the pre-Reformation faith, and it was during the reign of Queen Elizabeth that two recusant priests – Robert Ludlam and Nicholas Garlick, a native of Dinting and former master of Tideswell Free Grammar School – were found hiding at Padley on 24 July 1588. All that has survived from the ruins is the old gatehouse and the chapel above. However, the chapel was reprieved from its secular abuses by the Roman Catholic diocese of Nottingham when it undertook restoration in 1932.

A Day in the Life of a Ranger

Northern District Ranger Ian Hurst on patrol, well equipped for any surprises that the unpredictable Dark Peak (inset) may have in store

It is just before 10 am on a Saturday at Fieldhead – the Peak National Park Information Centre and camp site at Edale, in the shadow of the Park's reigning peak, Kinder Scout. The campers are clearing up after breakfast and the first visitors off the early 'Ramblers Route' train from Manchester or Sheffield are cheerfully setting out for the hills with boots, anoraks and bulging rucksacks. Their heavy boots clomp loudly as they stride across the bare floor of the Information Centre to leave their route cards, or check on the latest weather forecast at the desk. A display on the wall warns them that Kinder is on the same latitude as Labrador or Siberia, and they are reminded that the modest 2,088ft mountain can still be a killer.

In a converted barn at the rear of the centre, another group of walkers is gathering. There is an insurance salesman, an engineer, and a couple of unemployed youths. Their equipment is a bit more worn than the average rambler's, but otherwise they are the same, itching to get on the hill. There is one difference, however, because they each wear a shining silver and green badge depicting Peveril Castle – the medieval stronghold of William Peveril, at nearby Castleton. They are part-time Patrol Rangers employed by the Peak National Park at weekends to provide the link between landowners, visitors and the Park authority. But there is much more to being a National Park Ranger than that, as a typical day was to show.

Full-time Ranger

Ian Hurst, Northern District Ranger, walks in – clad in the coveted lovat green sweater and twill breeches of a full-timer – to supervise the morning briefing. Malcolm Padley, a part-timer for nearly 30 years, information assistant and full-time litter warden (he is unofficially known as 'The Chief Womble') for the Park – chalks up the details of each ranger's patrol for the day on a blackboard at the end of the room. For Mike Morton, an architect from Stockport, his typical day will consist of an eight-mile round of Broadlee Bank, Jacob's Ladder, Edale Cross, the Woolpacks, Upper and Nether Tors and Golden Clough, returning to Fieldhead for five o'clock. A new member of the team doesn't understand one of Malcolm's abbreviations: '7-min crossing.' He explains it is rambler's shorthand for the quickest possible crossing of the five-square-mile Kinder plateau, between Mill Brook and Blackden Brook. 'You take the third grough to the east of Blackden Brook,' he says with a wisdom accumulated over many years of 'bog-trotting'.

Walkers are usually amiable, but for this school party the chat is informative as well as friendly

Ian, a full-time ranger for 16 years, explains there is an extra task for the Patrol Rangers today. They are engaged on a survey for the Park's consultant ecologist, which involves checking the effect walkers have on moorland vegetation. Each ranger is handed a map showing key points where he must stop, look around and count the number of walkers he can see in a particular area. 'Naturalists are concerned at the disturbance to wildlife which large numbers of walkers might be causing in moorland areas,' Ian says. 'We are also interested in finding out exactly where people go on the moorlands, to establish patterns of use.' The Peak National Park has 76 square miles of access land on the northern and eastern moors, where special agreements drawn up with the owners allow free access to walkers, subject to a commonsense set of bye-laws and closure for a few days each year during the grouse-shooting season (12 August to 10 December).

A thorough briefing session prepares Rangers for the prevailing problems and conditions 'on the hill'

The Peak Park's Ranger Service was set up one cold and wet Good Friday at a meeting outside the Nag's Head pub at Edale in 1954. This was the first ranger service to be operated in a British National Park, and its prime function was to patrol the newly-created access areas. In those days, the warden service – as it was known then – only covered the access areas, an important condition of the agreements. However, after local government reorganisation in 1974 it was expanded to cover the whole of the National Park.

Helping hands

There are four District Rangers, a dozen Area Rangers, and eight Seasonal Rangers on the full-time staff. They are backed up by about 170 part-timers and 200 volunteers, such as those assembled at Fieldhead. The Peak Park Conservation Volunteers are also part of the Ranger Service, and currently perform annually about 3,000 man-days of often back-breaking tasks. Ian's first job that day was to check on a group of volunteers at work in the delightfully-named Golden Clough, just up the Grindsbrook Valley from Edale.

As the others set off on their individual patrols, we walked up past the Nag's Head, a ramblers' pub since the days of 'Bloody Bill the Bog-trotter' – legendary landlord Fred Heardman, who set up the first informal National Park information centre in the snug. Just as we turn off the road to cross the Grinds Brook, an estate car pulls up. It is Bob Townsend, local tenant farmer and chairman of Edale Parish Council. Ian pauses to pass the time of day with him, and reflects on the unseasonably cold weather. Liaison with local people is just as important to the Ranger Service as helping visitors, for potential problems – such as a stray dog worrying sheep or a damaged stile or sign – can usually be solved by a friendly chat.

We said cheerio to Bob and set off over the famous Log Bridge, which is the start of a journey of a lifetime for thousands of ramblers as they embark on Tom Stephenson's epic 250-mile Pennine Way. As we stepped on to the bridge, Ian paused and turned to lift what appeared to be a loose board. Underneath he revealed a pressure-counting device which, even at that early hour, had recorded the passage of nearly 50 walkers. Over the bridge, we climbed a rustic staircase which by-passes the original route of the Pennine Way, fenced off several years ago to halt the erosion caused by thousands of pairs of vibram-soled walking boots. The area is now green again, and sapling trees are thriving. 'Human erosion is a big problem in popular areas like Grindsbrook,' explains Ian. 'We do what we can to try to repair badly-eroded areas and enhance the landscape.'

A few yards up the meadow beneath The Nab we came across a length of rough gritstone cobbles, where the Way had been experimentally paved for a short stretch. It gave easy, dry walking for a few yards, whereas on either side the footpath has been worn into four, five or even six muddy lanes – the infamous 'Pennine Motorway'. 'If we had the manpower and resources, I'd like to provide this sort of well-drained paved surface over all the most badly-eroded sections in lowland situations like this,' says Ian.

Making good

Passing through a scraggy plantation of trees, we came to the kissing gate leading down to Golden Clough. The band of workers from the Derbyshire Conservation Volunteers, based in Derby, were hard at work reconstructing the footpath and drystone wall alongside the bubbling waters. It was a grand setting, with the sharply-pointed peak of Ringing Roger looking like a miniature Matterhorn at the head of the cascading clough. The volunteers were being supervised by Jeremy Brown, Seasonal Ranger and volunteers' organiser. He and Ian discussed progress. The long length of gritstone wall which led down the valley was in a sad state of repair, and the young volunteers were engaged on intricate and laborious reconstruction.

There was some discussion on whether the wall should be 'battered,' that is, smoothly-sloped down following the contours of the clough, or stepped. Ian surveyed the scene. 'We don't expect contractor's standards of walling from volunteers, but we must try to get the best job we can. It is often a case of horses for courses, and we try to match people to the kind of jobs they can do. There's no doubt that if it wasn't for the volunteers, many jobs just wouldn't get done at all. The bonus is that the youngsters from the surrounding cities and towns who come out in these work parties are learning a lot about the countryside and countryside skills.' Other volunteers are wielding picks and shovels, and clearing the ground for an improved set of steps up from the clough and its wooden bridge where the Pennine Way starts its long climb into the Grindsbrook Gorge, towards Kinder Scout. A huge flat boulder from higher up at 'Bungalow Corner' was transported down, balanced precariously on a wheelbarrow, surrounded by willing hands. It will end up as one of the Golden Clough steps.

The day, which had started out bright and sunny, had now deteriorated and the 'clag' (as the mist and clouds are known here) had descended over the head of the valley. Kinder had been beheaded by shifting mist carrying a fine, penetrating rain. It was turning into a typical Kinder day, and those who were tempted by that early-morning sun to head for the heights would now be enveloped. The mountain was showing its other, malevolent face, always ready to catch out the unprepared.

Ian Hurst's district covers about 150 square miles of these brooding, desolate moors, from Castleton in the south to Marsden in the north. He is constantly on call as a mountain-rescue controller, and the base at Fieldhead which we left that morning doubles as a mountain-rescue post. 'We get an average of about one call-out a week,' says Ian. 'Many of our Rangers are members of the local mountain-rescue teams, and as co-ordinator I have to liaise closely with the police and the other emergency services.' His radio call-sign, 'Peakland India' has been busy on the rescue frequencies during the past year, after a severe winter which stretched physical and material resources to the limit. A group of girls on a Duke of Edinburgh Award expedition went missing on the bleak Howden Moors, and a huge sweep search was instituted, involving two helicopters. Fortunately, they were found – lost, but safe and well. Ian also had to evacuate a young lad off the dangerous face of the so-called 'Shivering Mountain' of Mam Tor, near Castleton, after he had ventured too far on to its shifting shales. Ian has done some climbing, but does not regard himself as an expert.

Anyone who has experienced the isolation of the high moors will appreciate why radio links are a must

It is not only people who have to be rescued. A couple of years ago the Rangers were involved in an extraordinary series of rescues when Ian was stationed in the West and Central District. On successive weeks, he was called on to retrieve sheep from a ledge on a vertical limestone cliff in Water-cum-Jolly Dale, above the rushing waters of the River Wye. On both occasions the sheep had strayed and slipped down on to the ledge, from which there was no way back. 'The funny thing was, we think it was the same sheep both times,' recalled Ian, who received an RSPCA commendation for his action in retrieving the animal. It was sheep again, during the last bitter winter, which had to be rescued as they became buried by the score in mountainous snowdrifts whipped up by the biting winds. The Park's Ranger Service was praised by police and farmers alike for the Herculean efforts they put in to assist both man and beast in the atrocious conditions. Many sheep died, but many others were saved as they were dug out or fed by teams of Rangers working round the clock.

It is not only in winter that the emergency service provided by the Rangers is called on. High summer can be a time of severe pressure too, when the peat-covered moors can quickly turn as dry as the proverbial tinder box. A carelessly-discarded match, cigarette end or even broken glass is enough to ignite the peat into a raging fire which, because of the nature of the material, can burn for weeks. Ian recalled the aerial fire-spotting exercise he was involved in during the dry summer of 1980. 'As we flew over the area, it looked as if the whole place was going to go up in flames.' Fire-fighting on a peat moor is a thankless task. Surprisingly, a moor which is a waterlogged bog in the winter can turn into a dust-ridden desert after a spell of hot, dry weather, and water is often a long way from the seat of the fire. Five-gallon backpacks weighing 50lbs or more are used to carry water and a herbicide-type spray nozzle to the fire, and it is usually a long, hot and dusty walk to the nearest hillside spring. Nowadays, the service also has the multi-purpose Argocat vehicle to help transport water and men to the scene of a fire. This eight-wheeled, go-anywhere vehicle has greatly assisted in the logistical problems in both summer and winter – when fodder was taken to stock – but the Rangers only have one.

Long commitment

Ian has a strong sympathy for the farming community, for after he left school in Sheffield he spent some time in working on local farms in the Bradfield area. His introduction to the Ranger Service was as a young lad of 15 or 16, when he saw a man wearing the distinctive armband while he was out walking near Kinder Downfall – the spectacular waterfall which gave Kinder Scout its name. 'I saw this chap representing the National Park – and I have a strong suspicion it was Malcolm Padley – and I thought to myself, I'd like

to do that.' He took his warden training-course certificate in 1963 and became a Patrol Warden at the age of 21, based at Stanage on the Eastern Edges. Later, he became a full-timer and moved to Crowden-in-Longdendale in 1970 as an assistant warden. Such is the attraction of a Ranger's outdoor life that when Ian left Crowden on promotion as District Ranger for the West and Central District in 1977, there were over 1,000 applications for his job, from clergymen to high-flying young executives. Ian knows he is in a job which is the envy of many, although he is equally sure that if they knew the salary and the unsociable hours which he has to put in, many would also have second thoughts at the prospect.

'I thoroughly enjoy the life,' confessed Ian as we headed back down to Edale in the steady drizzle. 'But like any other job, it has its good and bad sides. For most visitors and local people we *are* the National Park, for we are likely to be the only representatives they meet in the field. Therefore we have to be Rangers, ready to solve little local problems; information officers, helping and directing visitors, and sometimes even the link with the planners back at the Park headquarters.

'I never try to force myself on people, although most folk on the hill will want to speak as you pass. We are there to give help if required, but we are not there to impose ourselves or the authority on people, most of whom are either out just to enjoy this marvellous scenery, or getting on with their own lives as farmers or local residents.'

A message on the wall of the Fieldhead briefing centre from 'a satisfied customer' puts it succinctly: 'Above 2,000ft, the most comprehensive social service in the country.'

No matter how good they are with maps and compass, walkers are always comforted by the waymarks sited even in remote places by the National Park Rangers

Gazetteer

▲ Thorpe Village Church

Each entry in this Gazetteer has the atlas
page number on which the place can be
found and its National Grid reference
included under the heading. An
explanation of how to use the National
Grid is given on page 78.

ALSTONEFIELD

MAP REF: 94SK1355

Alstonefield stands at 900ft between the Dove and Manifold, and 150 years ago it was a huge parish embracing all the land between the two rivers. Although much reduced it still remains large, and includes the hamlet of Milldale – at the northern end of Dovedale – among other scattered settlements. Its site is at the junction of several ancient tracks, later to become packhorse ways, and in 1308 it received a charter for the market that continued there until 1500. Annual cattle sales were held in the yard of the George Inn right up until early this century.

Spurned by canal and railway engineers for sound geographical reasons, Alstonefield lies some 2 miles from the nearest classified road and is today a charmingly unspoiled village. Several of its mullion-windowed houses form a delightful group with the George around the village green, between which and the church is the Hall – formerly the Rectory – of 1587. Behind this is a tithe barn, featuring an internal wall of exposed wattle and daub and a spiral stone staircase, which may have belonged to its predecessor.

There has been a church at Alstonefield since at least 892, but the earliest parts of the present building – the Norman south doorway and chancel arch – date from around 1100. The remainder is a mixture of the Decorated and Perpendicular styles, with a profusion of 17th-century woodwork including box pews and a two-decker pulpit of 1637. Both features were by a local man called Edward Unsworth.

The elaborate grey-green pew belonged to the Cottons of Beresford Hall – birthplace of Izaak Walton's friend Charles Cotton, who wrote the second part of *The Compleat Angler*. Although the hall was demolished in 1858, the fishing temple built by Cotton to entertain Walton survives on private ground in Beresford Dale.

ARBOR LOW

MAP REF: 92SK1663

Having walked through a farmyard and up a sloping field to reach the Peak's largest stone circle, the visitor may be momentarily disappointed to find that the 47 perimeter and three central stones are all recumbent. However, the fascination of this impressive

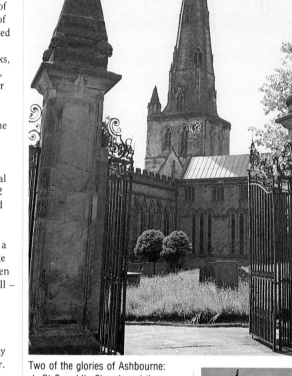

Two of the glories of Ashbourne:
▲ St Oswald's Church and the
Grammar School ▶

monument from the late Neolithic and early Bronze Age period – dating from around 2,000BC – quickly exerts its undeniable presence.

It has the usual henge features – a 250ft-diameter circular bank and 30ft-wide ditch, with two entrance causeways across them. At the centre of this enclosure is the 150ft-diameter circle of stones, near the middle of which excavations in 1902 discovered remains of a man who had been buried without the grave goods that would normally have been included to ease his transition into the next world. Relics found in an early Bronze Age barrow on the bank in a stone cist, or small burial chamber, included cremations, a bone pin and two food vessels.

A contemporary linear earthwork is visible for about 200yds south of Arbor Low, while some 350yds south-west of this feature on 1,150ft Gib Hill is Peakland's largest round barrow. Excavations near its top in 1848 revealed a cist containing a cremation and a food vessel.

ASHBOURNE

MAP REF: 80SK1846

Although this attractive little market town straggles along Henmore Brook a mile or so south of the National Park boundary, it is a good centre from which to explore the valleys of the Dove and Manifold – and indeed, the whole south-western corner of the Peak. In a sense it is a frontier town between lowland Britain to the south and the more rugged landscape of highland Britain in the north. Most of its buildings are of typical Midland red brick, but a sprinkling of stone reminds the visitor of the Peak's proximity.

The *Esseburne* of *Domesday* was a small settlement sited north of the Henmore, around an already ancient church. Immediately to the east, a 13th-century lord of the manor laid out a new town with a long main street, large triangular market place and parallel building plots – or 'burgages' – stretching to back lanes. A market charter was obtained in 1257.

To avoid paying the town's tolls while enjoying its benefits, some traders built themselves houses south of the brook in what became the suburb of Compton, which was eventually absorbed into the town.

Ashbourne developed slowly until its 18th-century coaching heyday, when it became a fashionable social centre. Many of its best buildings were built or refaced in the Georgian era, and some of the finest of them can be seen in Church Street and St John Street.

At the western end of this 'double' street is the splendid cruciform Parish Church of St Oswald, described by George Eliot as the 'finest mere parish church in England'. Capped by the tallest spire (212ft) in the Peak District, it contains Thomas Banks' famous monument in Carrara marble to Penelope Boothby, who died aged five in 1793.

Also at the western end of the street is The Mansion, a late 17th-century house refaced in the 1760s for Dr Johnson's oldest friend, the Rev Dr John Taylor. Dr Taylor lived here in considerable style on an income derived from various benefices, which he rarely visited. Almost opposite is the Grey House, which has a finer Georgian frontage and once belonged to an innkeeper who eventually owned the Buxton baths. Next door is the

▲ Well dressing: Ashford

original stone-built Grammar School – founded by Queen Elizabeth I in 1585, completed by 1606 and visited by Queen Elizabeth II on the occasion of its four-hundredth anniversary.

Spanning St John Street is the rare 'gallows' inn sign of the Green Man and Black's Head Royal Hotel, a name commemorating the amalgamation of two coaching inns in 1825. James Boswell found the Green Man 'a very good inn' and its landlady 'a mighty civil gentlewoman'. A recently restored timber-framed shop close by makes the traditional Ashbourne gingerbread, reputedly to a recipe acquired from French prisoners detained in Ashbourne during the Napoleonic Wars.

A better-known Ashbourne tradition is the annual football game played through the streets and along the Henmore on Shrove Tuesday and Ash Wednesday

between teams of no set number, nominally representing the 'Up'ards' and the 'Down'ards' – the brook being the dividing line. Its history, like its rules and skills, has long been forgotten; but it is great fun (except perhaps for property owners), and numerous attempts to ban it have all been rightly thwarted.

ASHFORD IN THE WATER

MAP REF: 92SK1969

On occasion this delightful place-name has been all too accurate, but normally the pellucid waters of the trout-filled River Wye keep to their channel between the houses, and away from the bypass which takes the A6 round the elegant village itself.

'Sheepwash' is the oldest, narrowest and most picturesque of several bridges spanning the Wye here. Originally for packhorses but now closed to all traffic, it takes its name from an adjacent stone enclosure in which sheep used to be washed – and occasionally still are for demonstration purposes.

Holy Trinity Church preserves four white paper garlands, or 'virgin crants', which used to be carried at the funerals of unmarried girls.

Ashford, which dresses six wells, has numerous 18th-century buildings and a few from the 17th – including a tithe barn now serving as an art gallery, and the largely unspoilt Devonshire Arms.

Sheepwash Bridge at Ashford in the Water spans the tree-shaded Wye. Its 17th-century fold is still used for washing sheep ▼

UNDERGROUND RICHES

Many of the thousands of tourists who flock to Castleton annually come away with souvenirs made from a unique mineral found in the hills surrounding the little township at the head of the Hope valley.

The beautiful blue, purple, yellow and white-banded fluorspar known as Blue John is a Castleton speciality, found only in Treak Cliff – the limestone hill which stands between the village and Mam Tor. It was formed millions of years ago when waves of hot minerals from the earth's core surged up between cracks and fissures in the limestone which, in places like Treak Cliff, was impregnated by natural oils or hydrocarbons. When these molten solutions cooled, they were transformed into the banded crystals of fluorspar.

The name is thought to come from the French *bleu-jaune* meaning 'blue-yellow', or it may have been adopted by the early lead miners to differentiate it from 'black-jack', their name for zinc-blende.

There is a persistent local legend that Blue John was first worked by the Romans, but this is perhaps based on the fact that two vases made of similar fluorspar were unearthed during excavations at Pompeii. There is no real evidence that they came from Castleton.

The first accurate record of Blue John was not made until the late 17th century. From the middle of the 18th century the Midland engineer Matthew Boulton used Blue John as a foil for ormolu (gilded bronze) in the ornaments he created for many stately homes. Later, Robert Adam used it as an inlay for fireplaces at Kedleston Hall, near Derby. In 1768 Boulton unsuccessfully tried to obtain a monopoly of the Blue John

▲ Treak Cliff's Blue John stone

mines, which at their height produced 20 tons annually.

Today that figure is down to only about half a ton, and the mineral is found in veins averaging only 3in in thickness – making it only suitable for jewellery and small ornaments. Visitors can still see veins of Blue John, of which 14 types are recognised, in the Blue John and Treak Cliff Caverns. The best of the Treak Cliff chambers were accidentally discovered in 1926, when miners searching for Blue John blasted their way into the beautifully decorated inner caverns.

Another bituminous impurity in the limestone created Ashford Black Marble, which was in much demand during Victorian times as a material for *objets d'art*. Really a compact and finely textured grey limestone, the 'marble' is created by fine polishing of the cut surface, which gives it a brilliant, satin-black appearance.

Black marble from the mines in the Ashford in the Water district was used for clock cases, candlesticks, book-ends, inkstands and miniature obelisks. It was also sought after for intricate inlays in table tops, murals and fireplaces in the homes of the well-to-do. The stone can be found at both Hardwick Hall and Chatsworth.

Unlike Blue John, Ashford Black Marble has a record of exploitation which goes back into prehistory, for pieces of dressed marble have been found in burial mounds nearby.

Exploration should begin in the main village, where the church interior is as rewarding as the setting and its 15th-century tower and spire suggest. In particular, the alabaster tomb-chest with effigies of Thomas Babington (died 1518) and his wife has been called 'the best in Derbyshire'. Surprisingly, the Norman font is the only lead one in a lead-producing county of which Ashover was a centre. The association is obvious from the memorials on the walls – note especially the one 'in Memory of David Wall, whose superior performance on the Bassoon endeared him to an extensive musical acquaintance . . .'

Next to the church is the Crispin Inn, which claims (dubiously) to date from 1415 – the year of Agincourt. It more likely dates, like many other buildings in the parish, from the 17th century. The whole village is worth exploring, and in places it is possible to follow the track of the Ashover Light Railway. This friendly little line was built to take lime from Ashover to Clay Cross Works, but between 1925 and 1959 it also provided a passenger service between the village and the main line at Stretton.

Surrounding hills – especially High Ordish or Cocking Tor – provide splendid views over Ashover and along the valley of the River Amber, on the banks of which the village stands.

AXE EDGE
MAP REF: 91SK0370

This long, gritstone escarpment rises to 1,807ft and is one of Peakland's grandest viewpoints. The A53 Buxton-to-Leek road following its eastern flank offers a spectacular drive – while the A54 Buxton-to-Congleton highway to the west is scarcely less dramatic. Axe Edge Moor, which lies between the two, is strictly for hardy walkers. It receives over 50in of rain annually, and the snow often lingers long into spring.

Not surprisingly, it is a watershed and the source of five important rivers. The Dove and Manifold rise close together just east of the A53, and after following almost parallel courses join forces at Ilam to flow south-eastward into the Trent and thence to the North Sea. About 2 miles north, the Wye rises above Buxton to run south into the Derwent and eventually into the Trent. The Goyt, however, rises just west of Axe Edge and flows north to become one of the main sources of the Mersey. There it is

ASHOVER
MAP REF: 81SK3463

This sprawling collection of scattered settlements covers almost 10,000 acres and is a place of charm and quirky character, built almost entirely of stone quarried from hills within the parish.

◄ The fine old Peakland market town of Bakewell lies on the banks of the Wye joined by the Dane, which has run south and then west around the Cheshire Plain from a source less than 2 miles from the head of the Goyt.

Close to the Goyt's source on the A537 Buxton-to-Macclesfield road is the solitary Cat and Fiddle Inn, which at 1,690ft is the second highest inn in England – after Tan Hill Inn between Swaledale and Teesdale. On the Leek road are the Traveller's Rest at just over 1,500ft, and the Royal Cottage, just below 1,500ft.

Between the two is a minor road leading to Flash, which at 1,518ft proclaims itself to be England's highest village. That may make St Paul's Church (built 1744, rebuilt 1901) the highest parish church – in a non-doctrinal sense. A gang of coiners once operated in this remote spot – hence the term 'flash' for counterfeit money.

BAKEWELL

MAP REF: 92SK2168

Bakewell has Derbyshire's second-busiest livestock market. It is also the headquarters of the Peak Park Joint Planning Board, whose Information Centre is housed in a splendid, converted 17th-century market hall in the town centre, where Bridge Street meets the attractive Market Place.

Badecean Wiellon ('Beadeca's Spring'), as the *Anglo-Saxon Chronicle* called it, sprang up at a natural crossing-point of the Wye – once guarded by a castle built by Edward the Elder in 942. Already a sizeable royal manor by the time of the *Domesday* survey, it had a market, confirmed by a charter in 1330 and banished from the streets to its present site in 1826.

In 1086 Bakewell, at the centre of a vast ecclesiastical parish, was the only settlement in the area with two priests. Traces of the Saxon church remain, as do the well-preserved stumps of two Saxon crosses in the hillside churchyard, and fragments of others in the south porch. The tower and spire that dominate the town are mainly the result of a 19th-century rebuilding programme, the rest of the church being an intricate mixture of all periods from the 12th century onwards. The various works are extremely well labelled and interpreted for the benefit of visitors. Not to be missed are the monuments in the Vernon chapel, including that of Dorothy Vernon and her husband John Manners (see Haddon Hall).

That applies equally to the Old House Museum farther up the hill in Cunningham Place. As interesting as the admirable local folk collection is the early Tudor house itself, and the story of its restoration after rescue from threatened demolition.

Probably equally old are the houses of Avenel Court, below the church in King Street, though they are disguised behind a 1780 shop front. In the same square (known as the Butter Market) is the Old Town Hall of 1684. Originally the upper floor only was used, with almsmen housed below until the row of almshouses behind was added in 1709. Bakewell is full of good old buildings deserving of inspection. Many date from around 1700 when the Duke of Rutland was trying to establish a spa here – unsuccessfully, because the water was colder than that at Buxton. The Bath House of 1697 and Bath Gardens are survivals from that time.

Along the A6 on the town's northern edge, close to Arkwright's Lumford Mill (established 1777), a typically low-parapeted packhorse bridge of 1664 spans the River Wye. The town bridge is more than 300 years older. Rainbow trout and ducks queue up to be fed from the riverside walk below.

BAKEWELL PUDDINGS

If you don't want to upset the locals in Bakewell, just be careful how you refer to their most famous homemade delicacy. Mr Kipling may call his version 'tarts', but you'll get some black looks if you ask for them by that name in the town of their origin. In Bakewell they are *always* known as 'puddings' which is, in any case, a more accurate description of this unique sweet which now carries the name of the Peakland 'capital' all over the world.

The story of the Bakewell Pudding is one of a disaster which turned into a delicacy. According to tradition, the first Bakewell Pudding was created by mistake by a flustered cook at the former White Horse Inn, in Matlock Street, around 1860.

Mrs Greaves, the landlady of the inn, issued instructions for her cook to prepare a strawberry tart for some important guests. The cook, in the hustle of a busy kitchen, mistakenly put the jam in first and then poured in the egg mixture designed for the pastry on top. The resulting sweet-

tasting pudding, far from being a disaster, was voted an instant hit by the distinguished guests and became a regular item on the inn's menu by popular demand.

When the cook, whose name unfortunately has been lost to posterity, made her will, she wrote down the fortuitous recipe. Who was left with the original, 'real' version of the instructions is still a matter of much local dispute and rivalry, for two local bakeries which make puddings claim the privilege.

The Old Original Pudding Shop in Bridge Street was built in the late 17th century and, despite its name, started life as a chandler's shop making candles. Mrs Wilson, the wife of the chandler, is said to have first seen the commercial possibilities of the puddings, and obtained the recipe. The other claimant of the original recipe is the bakery in Matlock Street, which was said to have been given it by the man who helped the cook write her will.

Even today, the actual mixture remains a closely-guarded secret, although the ingredients are fairly common knowledge: eggs, butter, strawberry jam, flaky pastry and a hint of almond essence. The result, a fairly ordinary-looking dish, is now taken all over the world by tourists who visit the pretty market town by the Wye – and some puddings are even sent by post!

▲ Eagle Stone at Baslow Edge commands magnificent views

BAMFORD
MAP REF: 88SK2083

Although its railway station is on the Hope valley line, Bamford village lies farther north up the Derwent, clinging to the steep lower slopes of Bamford Edge above the river. A cotton mill established there around 1780 burnt down within a decade – like so many others – and was rebuilt in 1791. After closure in 1965 it was turned to the production of electric furnaces. William Butterfield designed the church, with its unusual tower and spire, when Bamford became an independent parish in 1860.

A hill-farming village, Bamford is well-known for its annual sheep dog trials on the late spring bank holiday. It is also noted for its popular inns, and its position as the last village south of the spectacular Derwent reservoirs.

Immediately west of Ashopton viaduct a good, unclassified road runs up to the head of Howden, but at busy times there are restrictions on cars beyond the Fairholmes parking area and information point, as in the Goyt valley. A minibus is provided and cycles may be hired there.

Dr Barnes Wallis used the awe-inspiring Derwent dam for his 'bouncing bomb' experiments during the hostile interlude of World War II, and much of *The Dambusters* was filmed on their wide waters.

▲ An unusual clockface and an imposing tower grace the church at Baslow

BASLOW
MAP REF: 93SK2572

South of the Hope valley runs the escarpment of the East Moors in a continuous series of razor-sharp 'edges', jagged with boulders, to form a natural eastern wall to the Derwent valley. At the northern end of stately Chatsworth Park, where the valley widens slightly to receive Bar Brook, is Baslow village. This is divided into three distinct settlements and sits prettily between the ridge and the Derwent River.

At Nether End is the private, north entrance to the park, with lodges by Wyatville (1840) and several hotels. Bridge End has a broach-spired church on the river bank. Its tower clock displays the name '*Victoria*' and the date '1897'

instead of numerals, an idea of the local Dr Wrench. A whip inside the church was once used by an official to drive out stray dogs during services. Close by is a 17th-century three-arched bridge, and a tiny tollhouse with a doorway only $3\frac{1}{2}$ft high – probably reduced in size when the level of the road was raised.

On Baslow Edge stands the Wellington Monument erected by Dr Wrench in 1866, a counterbalance to the Nelson Monument on Birchen Edge a mile away. The A621 Sheffield road passes between them beyond Far End, as it climbs to the exhilarating desolation of Big Moor and Ramsley Moor.

BEELEY

MAP REF: 93SK2667

Beeley, an estate village at the south end of Chatsworth Park, is missed by most tourists because its main street lies east of the Chatsworth road. Much of it was laid out by Paxton for the 6th Duke of Devonshire, rather in the style of Edensor village (see Chatsworth), but some buildings are older – including the early 17th-century Old Hall.

Beside the inn a minor road climbs to heather-clad Beeley Moor (1,200ft), where there are more than 30 prehistoric barrows and cairns. Hob Hurst's house, the traditional home of the goblin Hob Hurst, is a Bronze Age barrow which lies within a ditch and bank high on Harland Edge.

The numerous steep-sided narrow gullies criss-crossing the peat moors hereabouts are called 'sicks'.

BIRCHOVER

MAP REF: 93SK2462

In Birchover the village street climbs gently to Stanton Moor, the source of warm pinkish stone of which its houses were built. They were constructed 'by instalments, and with little regard to regularity', according to a visitor in 1848.

These instalments have taken place over a period of 300 years, but the vernacular style in the Peak has changed so little over the period that the houses blend together perfectly. The irregularity of siting, common among Peak villages, is caused by a shortage of level ground on which to build.

The two hospitable village inns were probably among the early 'instalments', with the Red Lion having grown over three centuries from a single 'houseplace' with a 30ft well, now under thick glass just inside the entrance. The Druid Inn, noted for its bar food, used to supply a guide to escort visitors

Primitive punishment: the village stocks at Birchover ▼

▲ Mysterious Rowtor Rocks are associated with the Druids

over nearby Rowtor Rocks – a somewhat superfluous exercise since the gritstone assembly rises to no more than 150ft and extends for a mere 80yds. Dimensions aside, it is as impressive as it is surprising, and despite legends of druidical origins it is actually the remains of an eroded ridge.

The caves and seats on Rowtor were carved out by an eccentric clergyman, the Rev Thomas Eyre, who died in 1717. He liked to sit on the rocks composing sermons for delivery in the little chapel below – where nowadays can be seen extraordinary wood carvings, primitive wall paintings, modern stained-glass windows and a war memorial pulpit (1949), the work of modern and equally creative incumbents.

BONSALL

MAP REF: 93SK2858

This hillside village is just as irregular and engaging as Birchover, the major difference being that it is built of an almost white local limestone and features gritstone mullions, door-jambs and lintels.

From the Pig of Lead Inn the village street climbs 450ft to Upper Town, which is 850ft above sea level and just below the rim of the limestone plateau. Halfway up is a tiny market place, with a medieval stone cross on a circular base of 13 steps. Its shaft was renewed in 1871. Overlooking it is the King's Head, established in 1677 by Anthony Abell, and close by in High Street is the roughly contemporary manor house. Even the parish church is on split levels, which makes it accessible only by numerous steps.

Bonsall was once a stocking-making village, and one or two tiny workshops remain amongst the pigeon lofts. It was even more a lead-mining centre and the plateau is a honeycomb of miners' tracks and mine shafts. Most of the excavations have been capped, but care is still needed by anyone walking there – perhaps searching for the source of the little Bonsall Brook which dictated the shape of the village and turned the wheels of many mills in Bonsall. Along the tree-lined Via Gellia valley road to Cromford it supplied some of the power for Arkwright's mills. Between the two villages, it also supplied power for the original Viyella mill – which took its name from the Via Gellia, built in the 1790s by Philip Gell of Hopton Hall for the carriage of lead and stones from his mines and quarries to the Cromford Canal terminus.

BRADBOURNE

MAP REF: 95SK2152

Dunstable Priory grazed 1,200 sheep in the hills around Bradbourne seven centuries ago. For more than 300 years they also supplied monks as vicars of a church whose main features remaining today are fragments of Saxon work, three Norman doorways and a thick-set west tower of the same period, with a later stairway turret.

There are fine views to the south and north-west from this hilltop churchyard, which contains the shaft of a Saxon cross (*c.* 800) and the grave of Nat Gould. Nat Gould's working life began on his uncle's farm opposite and ended in 1919, after he had written 130 horse-racing novels in 25 years. Noticeably lacking in both church and churchyard is a war memorial; this is because all the Bradbournians in active service during both World Wars returned home safely.

East of the church, Bradbourne Hall is a handsome, stone, mainly Elizabethan manor house. Facing the road, the Old Parsonage is built in styles of three different periods, in different materials. Cottages of nearly white rubble-limestone add to the attraction of this small, unspoilt village immediately outside the park's south-eastern boundary.

▲ Beaks, birds and animals embellish the south doorway of All Saints, Bradbourne

BRADFIELD

MAP REF: 85SK2692

From the A57 Snake Pass road, the first (or last) northward unclassified lane east of Ashopton viaduct leads over an enchanted countryside of wild moorland and deep, green valleys to the village of Bradfield. On the way it passes the reputedly 14th-century Strines Inn and runs close to the expansive Strines and Dale Dike reservoirs.

Both the feel of the country and the architecture of the rare buildings are different from those of the Derbyshire and Staffordshire Peak Districts. If any more confirmation is needed, the superb cricket ground round which Low Bradfield seems to have been built confirms that this is Yorkshire.

Bradfield is sited at 860ft in a sheltering fold of high moorland above the Loxley valley, nestling round a splendid castellated, pinnacled and much-gargoyled church in a situation that would seem utterly remote but for urban-type bus-stop signs, which remind visitors that the urban sprawl of Sheffield is just 7 miles away.

A mere chapel-of-ease until 1868, St Nicholas is among the largest and grandest Peakland village churches, owing its opulence to Ecclesfield Priory – which built it and provided its early priests. Dating chiefly from the late 15th century, it has a 14th-century tower and preserves fragments of Norman work from an earlier building. Superb views from its south porch span the valley, over the Agden and Damflask reservoirs to the moors beyond. The eye is also attracted downwards to a patchwork of walled fields – the original broad-field (or fold) of the place name.

The Watch House, an oddly shaped Gothic private house, was built in 1745 for guarding against body snatchers who might be intent on plundering the adjoining churchyard. The village stocks and a double horse trough are nearby, while at the edge of a wood west of the church are traces of a motte-and-bailey castle. Another motte can be seen farther east.

Sheffield Viking Sailing Club has its headquarters on Damflask reservoir, which is also a popular picnicking spot.

BRADWELL

MAP REF: 88SK1781

Sandwiched by towering cliffs between Hope valley and Bradwell Dale, Bradwell is a place with lots of character and an industrial tradition. In addition to pursuing the usual Peakland extractive industries it has made lead miners' hard hats – known as 'Bradder beavers' – coarse-cotton goods, opera glasses, telescopes and umbrellas. It now has a vast cement works on its north-western edge and is a producer of excellent home-made ice-cream.

For the industrial archaeologist Bradwell's attractions are obvious, but the lay tourist makes for Bagshawe Cavern, which was discovered by lead miners in 1806 and is reached by descending 130 steps. The 'jitties' or 'ginnels', narrow passageways off the main road, are also worth exploring.

One mile south is Hazlebadge Hall, a former manor house (now a farm) dating from 1549. Brough, the same distance north, is a hamlet with a water-mill on the site of the Roman fort of *Navio* – of which nothing remains above ground.

BRASSINGTON

MAP REF: 95SK2354

This ancient lead-mining centre clings to the southern slopes of the limestone uplands just outside the Peak District National Park, its western boundary resting on a Roman road. Caves in the dramatic Harborough Rocks (½ mile east) have yielded finds from the Stone Age, and evidence of occupation in Iron Age and Roman times. As late as the 18th century Daniel Defoe encountered a cave-dwelling lead-mining family there.

Brassington Church is almost pure Norman, and a surprising number of solid Peak-style houses survive from the 17th and 18th centuries, when the mines prospered and the village stood on the main London-to-Manchester highway. The present post office was the last tollhouse on the Loughborough-to-Brassington road (turnpiked in 1738). The Gate Inn opposite takes its name from the turnpike gate, though the building itself dates from 1616.

Lead mines with names like Bees Nest, Innocent and Golconda mostly ceased production in the 19th century, though some have been briefly reopened since, in search of other minerals. Quarrying has continued in the area.

▲ Above: grey limestone cottages characterise the village of Brassington

Harborough Rocks, weathered into fantastic shapes, stand gaunt against the sky ▼

BUXTON

MAP REF: 91SK0673

A famous annual festival and the restoration of Buxton's main buildings has revived this one-time spa resort after a period of decline which affected most of its contemporaries during the mid-20th century.

The Peak Rail Centre and the unique Micrarium – an exhibition of nature under the microscope – are among the new attractions in this tourist and conference centre. Older features that are still popular include Poole's Cavern – the reputed home of a medieval outlaw and the undisputed home of man in Romano-British times – and Grin Low Wood, designated a country park. Buxton Hall was rebuilt in 1670 and is now the Old Hall Hotel, probably the oldest building in this mainly Georgian and mid-Victorian town.

CALVER

MAP REF: 89SK2474

Stone-built Calver stands on the River Derwent, which is spanned here by a good 18th-century bridge now bypassed by a new structure carrying the main A623. Both are overlooked by an austerely handsome Georgian cotton mill – used today for other industrial purposes – which keen television addicts with long memories may recognise as Colditz Castle in the TV series, Colditz. A road heading past the mill, east of the bridge and through the village of Curbar on to Curbar Edge passes just north of a circular lock-up with a conical roof. It is well worth a second glance, as is the view from the nearby National Park property of Curbar Gap.

Buxton's Pavilion Gardens are colourful in all seasons ▼

BUXTON SPA

A kinder climate and a few feet lower in altitude, and Buxton might have become a spa to rival Bath or Cheltenham.

However, the climatic disadvantages associated with being the highest market town in England meant that the 5th Duke of Devonshire's 'Grand Design' to create a northern Bath was never realised.

Early travellers complained of Buxton's 'dreary hills', its 'dismal situation' and that it was 'liable to incessant rains from the height of the surrounding hills'.

The 1,000ft altitude was not enough to deter the spa-seeking Romans, however, who called their settlement Aqua Arnemetiae, which has been translated as 'the spa of the goddess of the grove'.

It was the constant 82 degrees Fahrenheit (28 degrees Centigrade) temperature of the pale blue, slightly effervescent waters from the eight thermal springs which attracted the Romans. Later, their apparently miraculous health-giving properties made them extremely popular with pilgrims, so much

Just west of Calver Bridge is the settlement of Calver Sough, which takes its name from the entrance to a drainage 'sough'. There are many such channels in the Peak, laid at enormous expense to free lead mines from water seeping through fissures in the limestone. A right turn by the traffic lights at Calver South leads through Froggatt village and on to Froggatt Edge, where there are 76 acres of National Trust woodland, meadow and pasture.

Both Curbar and Froggatt – nestling below their respective

so that Henry VIII ordered them to be closed.

By the time of Elizabeth I, the wells were again attracting so many that no 'dyseased or ympotent poore person living on Almes' was allowed in, unless they had a licence from two justices. Mary Queen of Scots, detained for many years at Sheffield and Chatsworth, was a frequent visitor who 'took the waters' for chronic rheumatism and other ailments. She wrote gratefully after her first visit: 'I have not been at all disappointed, thank God.'

The profits made from his copper mines at Ecton Hill in Staffordshire encouraged the 5th Duke of Devonshire to develop the lofty hill town into a spa. He appointed the architect John Carr of York to design the splendid Crescent, modelled on John Wood's Royal Crescent at Bath. The total cost of the superb, Doric-style building –

edges – are desirable residential villages much favoured by commuters, who can enjoy splendid walks and superb views along the valley and still be in their Sheffield offices within a comfortable 20 minutes. The edges are popular with rock climbers who enjoy many routes on the coarse gritstone.

CASTLETON

MAP REF: 88SK1583

Laid out as a planned town below the dominant Norman castle where Henry II accepted the submission of King Malcolm of Scotland in 1157, Castleton is unchanged in shape but is nowadays a village that has become a highly popular and thriving tourist centre.

Ruined Peveril Castle, in the care of English Heritage, has an original curtain wall showing early Norman herring-bone work on the north side – the only flank without natural defences. Henry II built the present keep 19 years after his triumph over Malcolm, and the gatehouse is also from the 12th century. The slightly later hall and circular towers are noteworthy for they contain Roman brick, probably from the remains of

▲ Chapel-en-le-Frith's bustling market place has an interesting medieval market cross and some ancient wooden stocks

which originally housed three hotels – was £120,000. It was finished in 1784.

The natural baths and St Ann's Well were also improved at this time, and in 1790, on the slope behind The Crescent, the Great Stables and Riding School were constructed to house visitors' horses. In 1858 the 6th Duke converted this building into a hospital, and in 1880 the circular central courtyard was enclosed by what is still the largest unsupported dome in the world, with a span of 154ft.

By the time of the 6th Duke of Devonshire, Buxton had developed into a fashionable health resort. He employed Sir Jeffrey Wyatville to design the elegant parish church, and to lay out the graded paths of The Slopes.

The long-awaited coming of the railway in 1863 marked the zenith of Buxton's popularity. The imposing Palace Hotel of 1868, the Pavilion and Pavilion Gardens of 1871 and the ornate Opera House of 1905 – now the home of the international Buxton Festival of Music and the Arts – were all built to cater for the influx of visitors.

▲ Peak Cavern, or the 'Devil's Hole', one of seven Wonders of the Peak described by the philosopher Thomas Hobbes

Navio at nearby Brough.

Below the castle is the awesome mouth of Peak Cavern, about 50ft high and twice that wide, which once sheltered cottages and still harbours the remains of a ropewalk. From the mouth emerges a tributary of the Derwent, called Peakshole Water. Visitors have been enjoying guided tours of the cave for at least 300 years, which is about as long as the famous Blue John stone – a purplish-blue form of fluorspar – has been commercially extracted from lead workings in Treak Cliff.

The Blue John, Treak Cliff and Speedwell Caverns – all open to the public – are mixtures of natural cavities and lead-mine workings, with displays of stalactites and stalagmites similar to those found in Peak Cavern and other Derbyshire caves. Speedwell differs from the rest in that it is reached by a 104-step descent to a boat which is guided for about half a mile along an underground canal to a partly natural cavern, the working face of the former Speedwell Mine. Treak Cliff is virtually the only remaining viable source of Blue John.

St Edmund's Church, though heavily restored in 1837, retains 17th-century box pews, a fine Norman chancel arch, and a valuable library which includes a 1611 'Breeches' Bible. Possibly on a more pagan note, a popular event in the village calendar is the annual Garland Day. The curfew bell is still rung in Castleton church tower at 8 o'clock each night in the week, and the 'pancake' bell is still rung at 11am on Shrove Tuesday.

Overlooking Castleton is Mam Tor, also called the 'Shivering Mountain' because layers of soft shale between the harder beds of gritstone are constantly crumbling. From the village its 1,695ft bulk looks like a half-eaten apple. It has a Bronze and Iron Age fort on its summit. The A625 main road round the foot of the mountain has been permanently closed because of landslips, and traffic is now diverted up the Winnatts Pass. This steep, narrow defile between high limestone cliffs was once a coach road and nowadays is designated a Site of Special Scientific Interest.

Castleton Hall is a 17th-century house now serving as a Youth Hostel, while the 19th-century Losehill Hall is the Park Board's Residential Study Centre – the first of its kind to be set up by a National Park authority.

CHAPEL·EN·LE·FRITH
MAP REF: 87SK0680

As its name suggests, this town was originally a foresters' chapel in the Royal Forest of the Peak – a huge stretch of wasteland, not necessarily all wooded, reserved as a royal hunting ground.

By the time the present parish church replaced the chapel early in the 14th century, the area so designated was already dwindling, and in Charles II's reign it ceased to exist.

Chapel developed into a market town to which – about the turn of the century – it added vehicle-brake manufacture. This had curious origins in the footwear industry, which gave rise to the term brake 'shoes'. The cobbled market place (760ft above sea level) has a medieval market cross and stocks.

Two miles north-west, sandwiched between the massive bulk of Chinley Churn (1,480ft) and the conical-topped Eccles Pike (1,213ft), is the once-important Chinley railway junction. Although it has lost much of its former status, it has retained two magnificent stone viaducts.

A mile farther west is Buxworth, which is bisected by a bypass and features numerous relics of an earlier phase of the Industrial Revolution. Included are the terminal canal basin of the Peak Forest Canal – completed in 1800 by Benjamin Outram – and well-preserved remains of his Peak Forest Tramway. Operated partly by gravity, the tramway brought limestone and lime from the quarries and kilns 6 miles away at Dove Holes.

The village was called Bugsworth until the inhabitants, weary of the jokes, had its name officially changed in 1929. Bugsworth Hall, however, has proudly retained the old spelling, along with its gables and mullions of 1627.

▲ Early land enclosures produced Chelmorton's narrow fields

CHATSWORTH
MAP REF: 93SK2570

'Not so much a house as a town', the Duchess of Devonshire says of Chatsworth, but it is a very beautiful town. The first view of it across the park from the south is unforgettable. In the foreground – across the Derwent – the Emperor fountain sends up a 290ft jet of water, proclaiming itself the second-highest in Europe. East of the house water pours from jets in the Cascade House on the hillside, and tumbles over terraced steps before disappearing into the ground. Above that is thick woodland which climbs a steep cliff to the Hunting Tower, a gazebo built in Elizabethan times when Sir William and Lady Cavendish – 'Bess of Hardwick' – were laying out the first Chatsworth House.

The present mansion replaced it between 1678 and 1707. Dutch architect William Talman was employed by the 4th Earl to alter Bess's house in the classical manner, but the two styles proved to be incompatible. So did the Earl and Talman, who left. Later, the Earl, who became the 1st Duke in 1694, decided on a total rebuilding programme to his own designs – with advice and help from Thomas Archer. The only major change since then has been the addition of the north, or Theatre, wing by Sir Jeffrey Wyatville for the 6th 'Bachelor' Duke in 1820.

James Paine laid out the present road through the park in the 1760s. (The previous one ran east and west across the country.) He also built the two charming bridges, and the stables north of the house. Around the same time Capability Brown landscaped the park and altered the course of the river.

The estate village of Edensor (pronounced Ensor), which was formerly between the river and the road, was moved to its present site by the 6th Duke between 1838 and 1842. Sir Joseph Paxton – who was head gardener and almost managing director of Chatsworth, as well as an architect, writer and business tycoon – planned the village and designed some of the houses. The others are the work of J C Robertson, and no two are alike. Paxton also designed some of the houses in the estate village of Pilsley, to the west of the park, though a number of its buildings are older and date from the 18th century.

Chatsworth deserves a long, leisurely visit. It contains work by the finest craftsmen and artists, and its grounds are equally rewarding.

CHELMORTON
MAP REF: 91SK1170

By a Bronze Age tumulus on Chelmorton Low (1,440ft) rises a stream that is delightfully if inexplicably called Illy Willy Water. It was this which dictated the shape of the village – a single street with most of its farms strung along either side, their crofts laid out behind in the medieval style. Only six remain of the 20 or so that were once worked here. At the top of the street, just below the Low, is the medieval Church of St John the Baptist. Church Inn stands immediately opposite and early 18th-century Townsend Farm is the full-stop at the end of the village.

One of the most important things about Chelmorton is its pattern of 'fossil' arable strips within drystone walls enclosed by agreement from medieval times. Originally the complex was a single open field enclosed within an earth bank, part of which remains. Outside lay the common pasture. Beyond, stretching to the parish boundary, are neatly regular fields laid out by the Enclosure Commissioners after the 1809 Enclosure Award.

To quote from an official report, what the visitor sees here is 'an example of an historic landscape which is perhaps not seen to better effect anywhere else in Britain'. The Park Board is taking steps to ensure that it stays that way.

CHESTERFIELD
MAP REF: 81SK3871

Formerly a coal-mining centre and still a busy industrial area, Chesterfield is a lively red-brick town totally different in appearance and character from anywhere else in the Peak. It is also a good base from which to explore the eastern half of the National Park, and the start of a dramatic drive across the moors on the A619 to Baslow. Halfway along the road a stone wall separates green fields from brown moorland. No change could be more sudden.

Chesterfield has its own attractions. Best known and most obvious is the crooked spire of St Mary and All Saints Church, basically the result of incompatibility between lead and unseasoned timber – although there are more colourful explanations. The church itself testifies to the prosperity of the town, particularly its guilds, in the first half of the 14th century. Parts of the fabric date from a century earlier, and the building's size and grandeur – plus the importance of Chesterfield as Derbyshire's second town – only narrowly failed to win it cathedral status when the Derby Diocese was created in 1927. Inside are many fine monuments, particularly those of the Foljambe family at the east end of the Lady Chapel.

Local public opinion saved the spacious market place from redevelopment in the 1970s, and along with much more of the town centre it now forms part of a conservation area. Its most interesting building is probably the former Peacock Inn, which on the eve of demolition was found to be a medieval timber-framed structure. Probably the town house of a prominent local family, it has been restored as nearly as possible to its original form and is used as a heritage and information centre.

A leisurely inspection of Chesterfield above the modern shop fronts reveals a number of good old buildings of different periods, and some very presentable modern ones. Of particular note is the new County Library. Farther out in the northern suburb of Whittington, which has kept much of its original village core, is the much-restored, stone-built 16th-century Revolution House. Now a small museum, this was the inn where a number of aristocratic plotters – including the 4th Earl of Devonshire – planned the Great Rebellion of 1688, with the resultant abdication of James II in favour of William and Mary.

South-east of that is Tapton House, a late Georgian building which is now a school but was

The 14th-century crooked spire of St Mary and All Saints, Chesterfield, rises 228ft ▼

once the home of the great railway engineer, George Stephenson. Here in retirement he carried out experiments in horticulture, and one trade paper announced his death in 1848 under the headline, 'Inventor of Straight Cucumber Dies'. He was buried in Holy Trinity Church, Newbold Road, where the stained glass in the east window is a memorial to him.

CRICH

MAP REF: 81SK3554

George Stephenson owned both Crich Cliff Quarry and the gravity-incline railway that carried stone down a 1-in-7 slope from the cliff face to his battery of lime-kilns alongside the Cromford Canal, and to the Midland Railway in the Derwent valley. The last load was handled in 1957, and since 1959 the quarry floor has been occupied by the Crich Tramway Museum. Here trams that may once have clanged through the streets of Prague or Oporto carry visitors past Edwardian street advertisements, and out along a ridge which affords superb views.

Above the quarry, on Crich Cliff, is a light which shines out every night from the top of Crich Stand – a memorial tower 950ft above sea level which commemorates those soldiers of the Sherwood Foresters (the Nottinghamshire and Derbyshire Regiment) who fell in the two World Wars. The tower is

▲ Fun at Crich Tramway Museum

open daily, offering magnificent views extending from Lincoln Cathedral in the east to the Wrekin summit far away in the west. The tower stands on an island of limestone surrounded by gritstone.

The large, straggling hill village itself – once a market town, with a medieval market cross as evidence – has other surprises. Among the most picturesque is an 18th-century framework knitters' cottage of three storeys and a long upper window. Also interesting is a four-fold horse trough, probably for the packhorse teams which crossed these hills carrying lead and stone.

The Church of St Michael, partly Norman and with a Norman font, has a built-in stone lectern (rare outside Derbyshire), and some good monuments. One is to Sir William de Wakebridge (died 1369), who founded two chantries after losing his wife, father, two brothers and three sisters in the Black Death. Another recalls John Claye (died 1632), whose wife's father was 'unto that king of fame Henrie the Eight, chief cock-matcher and servant of his hawkes . . .'

Neighbouring Fritchley was an important Quaker centre in the 19th and early 20th centuries, and still has a flourishing Quaker chapel. It also has clear traces of a pre-Stephenson railway (or tramway), built around 1780 to take stone from another Crich quarry to lime kilns on the canal at Bull Bridge.

The Midland Railway Centre at Butterley station, 4 miles south-east of Crich on the outskirts of Ripley, caters for railway enthusiasts. Here there are passenger train rides, often behind steam locomotives, a developing railway museum – and another for other forms of transport – in a recently established country park.

CROMFORD
MAP REF: 93SK2956

Here in 1771 Richard Arkwright built the first successful water-powered cotton mill (see panel below) and added other mills during the next 20 years. The whole complex is gradually being restored by the local Arkwright Society. But this is by no means all there is to Cromford. The entire industrial village which Arkwright superimposed on a small existing hamlet is now a conservation area, notable for its well-preserved terraces of workers' cottages and for Arkwright's own two homes – pseudo-Gothic Willersley Castle, which was completed only just before his death in 1792, and Rock House, which looks down on his first mills and on the restored basin of the Cromford Canal. The former is now used as a Methodist guest house.

Along the Cromford Canal tow-path is Leawood Pump House, where a restored Watt-type beam-engine is periodically in steam. Just beyond the pump house is William Jessop's spectacular Wigwell aqueduct, which carries the canal high over the river valley.

Between Leawood and Cromford the canal passes High Peak Junction, once the terminus of the Cromford and High Peak Railway. Its restored workshops are now open to the public. Completed in 1831, this section of railway was the first line to cross the Peak from south-east to north-west, and

▲ There are pleasant walks along the towpath of Cromford Canal

WATER POWER

Cromford, just off the A6 as it approaches the Matlocks, has a spacious, urban air about it that is unusual in such an apparently quiet place. The broad market square is backed by the solid presence of the Greyhound Inn, and up The Hill towards Wirksworth, rows of neat, gritstone terraces give the impression of a carefully planned town.

The answer lies just across the A6 down Mill Lane, where the gaunt, fortress-like buildings of Upper Mill give the final clue to Cromford's past importance. For it was here that a 'bag-cheeked, pot-bellied Lancashire man' known as Richard Arkwright came in 1771 to build the first water-powered cotton mill, transforming textile manufacturing from a cottage to a factory industry.

It was the power of the River Derwent, which Daniel Defoe had called 'that fury of a river', and its tributaries which first brought the Preston-born barber and wig-maker to Cromford. Its very isolation, away from the prying eyes of competitors and close to a cheap, unorganised and plentiful supply of labour from the declining lead mines, must have been a major attraction.

Yet in the end, it was Cromford's isolation which was to prevent it becoming another Manchester. Poor communications and its distance from ports like Liverpool, where the raw cotton came in, eventually saw Cromford's decline – although Arkwright was to amass a personal fortune in 20 years which would allow him to boast he could liquidate the whole of the national debt.

Arkwright, the semi-literate genius who was the thirteenth child of a poor family, was to establish three mills in the village – and Masson Mill, built in 1784, was still used for textile manufacture until recently. Arkwright's planned township of Cromford was not his only work in the Peak District. Upstream on the River Wye he created Lumford Mill at Bakewell and Cressbrook Mill in Miller's Dale.

The 'furious river' and others like it had been used for centuries, of course, mainly for corn-grinding mills, but also for crushing mineral ores, pulping rags for paper, and even for grinding and polishing Ashford Black Marble.

One corn mill still grinds flour powered by the River Wye at Rowsley, where a dedicated band of enthusiasts operate Caudwell's Mill in much the same way as it has been for over a century. Remains of other corn mills still exist in Chatsworth Park (in ruins), at Over Haddon and Alport-by-Youlgreave. Bobbin mills at Ashford in the Water used the surrounding ash and sycamore woods as raw materials for another necessity in the textile trade.

Another fine old mill building, later to be used as a backdrop to the television series Colditz and now involved in the production of stainless steel products, is Calver Mill, built by John Gardom in 1804. Edale Mill, built in 1795 by Nicholas Cresswell, has been restored by the Landmark Trust, while Bamford Mill (1780), now produces electric furnaces and laboratory equipment.

Owners like Arkwright prided themselves on the provision they made for their workforces, which consisted mainly of women and children. Not all millowners were as benevolent, however, and the 1828 Memoirs of Robert Blincoe, employed by Ellis Needham at Litton Mill on the Wye, were a catalogue of cruelty and degradation. Modern scholars now believe they were 'ghosted' pieces of propaganda in support of long-overdue changes in factory laws.

▼ Arkwright's mills were the first to use water-driven machinery

was originally designed as a canal (the stations were called wharfs). Stationary engines hauled wagons up the steeper gradients, but locomotives operated on the more level portions. After its last section, the Middleton Incline (see Wirksworth) closed in 1967, the track was adapted as the High Peak Trail – a 17½-mile route for walkers, cyclists and horse-riders. Its first steep (1-in-7) incline climbs up to the Black Rocks, a gritstone edge popular with rock climbers, which has a picnic and parking area just off the Wirksworth road.

Near the canal basin the Derwent is spanned by a three-arched 15th-century bridge, with the ruins of a contemporary bridge chapel alongside. The early 18th-century fishing temple close by is a replica of the Walton-Cotton one in Beresford Dale.

DARLEY DALE
MAP REF: 93SK2762

A romantically minded vicar and the commercially minded Midland Railway Company have both been credited with devising this 19th-century name for the seemingly endless ribbon of buildings alongside the A6 north of Matlock – a sort of elongated centre for the collection of older and smaller settlements established east of the Derwent.

The name, the railway and the setting have in the past attracted both picnickers and commuters. Many of the former were from Manchester, and most of the latter were railwaymen – with the notable exception of Sir Joseph Whitworth, inventor of the screw thread. He bought Stancliffe Hall, built cottages for his estate workers, laid out new roads to ease his own passage to the station and eventually left to the village a hotel, an institute and a hospital named after him. All this had been intended to form the nucleus of a much larger model village.

For his development scheme Whitworth used stone from the nearby Stancliffe Quarry, a source of building material for fine architecture that included the Thames Embankment and Hyde Park Corner in London, and the Walker Art Gallery in Liverpool.

The medieval Parish Church of St Helen is a fine cruciform building standing in the hamlet of Churchtown, between the A6 and the river. In the churchyard are the ancient, battered remains of a once-huge yew tree, which is still

33ft in circumference when measured 4ft from the ground.

Nearby, 15th-century Darley Bridge carries the B5057 Winster road over the Derwent below isolated Oaker Hill (634ft), which is crowned by a single sycamore. North of the bridge are the remains of Mill Close Mine, the largest and most productive Derbyshire lead mine until flooding caused its abandonment in 1938.

DOVEDALE
MAP REF: 95SK1452

Possibly the most beautiful of all the Derbyshire dales – and thanks to Walton and Cotton, clearly the best known – Dovedale often hosts as many as 5,000 visitors on a sunny Sunday afternoon. Most tend to stay near the stepping stones, however, leaving the remaining 2½ miles uncluttered.

In its 45-mile course from Axe Edge to the Trent, the Dove is essentially a walker's river, almost inaccessible by car. This seclusion, along with its literary associations, the clarity of its tumbling water, its steep wooded sides, its white rocks carved into fantastic shapes by weather and water – and above all, the way it unfolds its beauty gradually, ever enticing the visitor on to see what lies beyond the next gracious curve – contributes greatly to the charm of Dovedale. At its end is Viator's Bridge and a short stretch of road to Lode Mill, then another 5 miles of enchantment woven by the magical Wolfscote and Beresford dales.

The main car park for Dovedale is below Bunster Hill, on the Staffordshire side of the river, which can be crossed either by bridge or the famous stepping stones. A smaller, newer car park is sited at Milldale, the only settlement anyone has managed to squeeze into the gorge. There is no long-term parking in Thorpe, the nearest village, except for residents at the hotel and guest houses. Accommodation began to spring up early in the 19th century, when a new enthusiasm for romantic scenery led to the area's 'discovery'.

Recently, more places to stay and cycle-hire facilities have been provided, but so discreetly that Thorpe remains a charmingly unsophisticated limestone village.

Its little church has a west tower, belfry windows and a font which are all of early Norman date. The early 14th-century nave has limestone rubble walls of various thicknesses, giving them the appearance of leaning outward, and the curious churchyard sundial is too tall to be read except from horseback. Beyond the church the village street degenerates into a track leading to 18th-century Coldwall Bridge, which has carried a green lane since having been deserted by its turnpike road when it proved too steep for traffic.

From the village a pleasant walk through Lin Dale leads down to the stepping stones below Thorpe Cloud ('clud' means 'a hill'), a much-climbed cone rising to 942ft. Like most of Dovedale, it is owned by the National Trust.

▼ Majestic Dovedale is one of the Peak's most popular beauty spots

EDALE

MAP REF: 87SK1285

Civilisation ceases at Edale. 'No turning space for cars beyond this point', says the sign at the top of the village. Beyond it the road stops and the skyline is jagged with the highest, wildest hills of the mysterious Dark Peak.

Here, at the Nag's Head, the Pennine Way starts its 250-mile northward journey to the Scottish border at Kirk Yetholm. Almost at once the route divides, one path heading north up Grindsbrook, and th other west up Jacob's Ladder to Edale Cross. They meet again by Kinder Downfall – the Peak's highest waterfall – on the 2,088ft boggy peat plateau of Kinder Scout. This is the highest point in the National Park.

Neither route, nor any other walk on the tops north of Edale, should be attempted without proper equipment and due heed to weather conditions. Sudden squalls, mists and dramatic temperature changes are features of this wild and dangerous country, where the going can be extremely tough.

Up-to-date weather and other information is always available from the National Park Information Centre at Fieldhead, between Edale church and the railway station. Maps and guides can be bought there too, and a permanent exhibition deals with the history of the area.

Edale began as a loose confederation of scattered settlements called booths, originally the 'bothies' or huts which give temporary shelter to shepherds and herdsmen tending their beasts on the summer pastures. Upper, Barber, Grindsbrook, Oller and Nether Booths became one parish, carved out of Castleton in 1863. By then Nether Booth had a cotton mill, which now serves as holiday accommodation and is owned by the Landmark Trust.

Otherwise, Edale has always been – and remains – a dairy-farming and stock-rearing area, to which tourism has been added since the arrival of the Sheffield-to-Manchester branch line in 1894. Those early visitors could only gaze at moors reserved for grouse and gamekeepers. That the Church Hotel became the Railway Hotel and is now the Ramblers' Hotel tells its own tale of Edale's changing priorities.

A former Nag's Head landlord – the late Mr Fred Heardman – and his customers began an unofficial mountain-rescue service which has grown into the Peak District Mountain Rescue Organisation. The inn was built in 1577, probably to serve drivers of packhorse teams carrying Cheshire salt across the Peak. A packhorse bridge still spans tumbling Grinds Brook just below the late 16th-century, mullion-windowed Waterside Cottage.

Besides its hotels, Edale has adventure and walking centres, camping and caravan sites, a large Youth Hostel, bed-and-breakfast accommodation and a residential youth centre at Champion House – run jointly by Derby Diocese and the Derbyshire County Council.

The only road to the village follows the course of the River Noe from Hope, then winds over Mam Nick. From this section there are magnificent views over the green Vale of Edale.

ELTON

MAP REF: 95SK2261

In Elton the main street follows a long, flat ledge where limestone and gritstone meet at over 900ft above sea level. On one side are lime-loving flowers and a few ash trees, and on the other gritstone vegetation thrives with a scattering of oaks. The houses reflect this dichotomy, some being of limestone, more of gritstone and the majority a mixture of each. This is seen to advantage in the many 17th- and 18th-century houses that survive – like the Old Hall, now a Youth Hostel, which is dated 1688. It has a more recent extension of 1715.

Although the surrounding countryside looks hard, water lies close to the surface and the land is good for rearing both sheep and cattle. It was also rich in lead, and until recently the villagers – as elsewhere in the uplands – practised the dual economy of mining and farming.

A mile north on Harthill Moor are curious outcrops of gritstone – like Robin Hood's Stride, which has terminal monoliths 22yds apart. Both it and Cratcliff Tor provide good rock-climbing. In a shallow cave at the Tor's foot, a medieval hermit carved out a crucifix, a stone seat and a niche for a candle.

The River Bradford rises one mile north-west of Elton at Dale End,

below Gratton Moor. This area, like Harthill Moor, is littered with prehistoric tumuli.

EYAM
MAP REF: 88SK2176

Infamous as a 17th-century plague village (see panel right), Eyam (pronounced 'Eem') is a large, almost self-contained and very typical mineral-mining and quarrying settlement with a fascinating history well documented by informative wall plaques and an excellent exhibition in the church.

In the churchyard are the Peak's best-preserved Saxon cross, an unusual sundial of 1775 and some interesting headstones – including a very English one to Derbyshire cricketer Harry Bagshaw. The church itself has been much restored, but its Saxon and Norman fonts, Jacobean woodwork and medieval wall paintings should be seen. Indeed, the whole village deserves careful study for its fascinating variety of local building styles.

The Vale of Edale
Inset: Eyam Church's sundial ▼

▲ Graves at Eyam tell their own story about the plague village

THE PLAGUE VILLAGE

Eyam is a busy, hard-working village nestling at the foot of Sir William Hill, above the limestone cliffs of Middleton Dale. The name, pronounced 'Eem', is thought to come from the Old English word meaning 'an island'. In the fateful years from 1665 to 1666, Eyam certainly *did* become an island, in what has been described as one of the most epic stories in the annals of rural life. The self-imposed quarantine of the tiny village when the dread plague virus arrived – so that the infection would not spread farther – has made Eyam a place of pilgrimage ever since.

Three centuries later there are still many poignant reminders in the village of those terrible days, when 259 people from 76 families died. Many of the houses where the killer disease struck still stand, and neatly painted signs give the names of the victims. Perhaps the most touching relic of those black days is to be found in a field about half a mile east of the village. There, in a lonely little walled enclosure known as the Riley Graves, are the simple memorials to a father, his three sons and three daughters – all of whom died within eight days of each other in August 1666. It must be presumed that they were all buried by the distraught mother. They were all members of the Hancock family, but tragedy had struck even harder at the neighbouring farm of the Talbots during the previous month, when a whole family of seven was wiped out.

It is thought the virus arrived at Eyam in a box of cloth brought from London by a journeyman tailor known as George Viccars,

who lodged with Widow Cooper in the cottages just west of the church. A few days later, on 7 September 1665, the first grim entry was made in the deaths register by the young rector William Mompesson, as Viccars was buried. A fortnight later one of Widow Cooper's sons, Edward, died of the same symptoms, and the following day a neighbour, Peter Halksworth, also succumbed.

Rumours of the deadly nature of the disease must have spread through the population like wildfire, but it was the young rector – aided by his non-Conformist predecessor Thomas Stanley – who united the villagers in their courageous decision not to flee, but to try to contain the outbreak within the community.

The decision was communicated to the Earl of Devonshire, the lord of the manor, who arranged for provisions, clothing and medical supplies to be left for collection at certain points around the village boundary, such as Mompesson's Well. Here coins were left in the water, disinfected with vinegar, as payment. Mompesson, having sent his own children away shortly after the outbreak, had the heart-rending task of burying his wife Katherine on 25 August 1666. Her table tomb is in the churchyard, near the ancient Saxon cross.

This touching and tragic story of the plague is remembered on the last Sunday of August every year, with a Commemoration Service in the open air at Cucklet Church, a natural limestone cavern where Mompesson held his services during the 'visitation' 300 years ago.

▲ Foolow's village green boasts a 14th-century stone cross

FOOLOW AND THE HUCKLOWS

MAP REF: 88SK1976

Foolow sits attractively round a large green – a rare Peakland feature – with a village cross, bull-ring and mere at the centre, and a well at the edge. Its lead mines have closed, though two mine hillocks are distantly visible. Commuters now occupy the farmhouses and their outbuildings, tastefully converted into 'desirable residences of character' – among them a pigsty and neighbouring cow-stall. The 18th-century Spread Eagle Inn is a private house too, though its tethering-rings for horses (the Georgian equivalent of a car-park) hint at its past. The Bull's Head (now renamed the Lazy Landlord) is the sole surviving pub of five that once stood here.

The Barrell Inn at Bretton, which has overlooked Foolow from 1,200ft on Eyam Edge since at least 1637, has been skilfully restored.

Camphill, 2 miles east of Bretton, on Hucklow Edge, is the headquarters of the Lancashire and Derbyshire Gliding Club. Venue of the 1954 World Gliding Championships, it is a place where visitors can watch gliding every weekend in the year, or join a five-day holiday course.

Below the Edge is Great Hucklow, 'great' only in comparison with Little Hucklow (2 miles north-west), and the closer Grindlow, having roughly half the combined population of about 260. Inspired by Laurence du Garde Peach, of *Punch* magazine, who lived nearby, it supported live theatre in an old lead-smelting works from 1927 to 1971. Audiences once travelled miles to the shows.

GLOSSOP

MAP REF: 82SK0394

A 10-minute car journey from Norfolk Square in Glossop is all that separates the town from the point between Featherbed Moss and Shelf Moor (1,670ft) where the Pennine Way crosses the A57 Snake Road. In winter this is often closed, but on good days it is an exhilarating drive. Over the central watershed the road follows the line of the medieval Doctor's Gate – named after a Dr Talbot, who rediscovered it – and drops down through Woodlands valley. From here it runs past the Snake Inn and accompanies the River Ashop until it widens into the Ladybower reservoir. It then crosses the Ashopton viaduct and continues to the city of Sheffield.

Glossop is an oddly civilised departure point for this drive over the wilderness, being an early 19th-century planned town, well laid out with dignified squares and public buildings for the 11th Duke of Norfolk. It stands at a point where three turnpike roads crossed the Glossop Brook. At that time the waterway had already been harnessed to provide driving power for machinery in three new cotton mills.

As an outlier of the then booming Lancashire cotton industry, the new 'Howardstown' outgrew the original village of Glossop and took its name when the municipal borough was formed in 1876. Old Glossop remains as an unspoilt, suburban enclave, containing a number of 17th-century houses.

One mile west of Glossop is the splendid Dinting Viaduct, and a farther mile north-west is the 19-acre fort site of Roman *Melandra*, on the edge of the vast, modern, Gamesley housing estate.

GOYT VALLEY

MAP REF: 90SK0172

The lovely upper reaches of the River Goyt (see Axe Edge) are best approached from Buxton and Long Hill (A5002) down a 1-in-7 gradient by Bunsall Incline – once the steepest on the Cromford and High Peak Railway. Motorists should tackle the few narrow lanes in the area with care, and never on Sundays or bank holidays when the valley road is closed – except to the car parks. The Goyt may have been 'little known to tourists', as a guide book said 80 years ago, but not now.

The valley has changed too, since Stockport Corporation dammed the Goyt to form two reservoirs – Fernilee in 1938 and Errwood in 1967. However, it is still beautiful in a slightly different way. In June the rhododendrons light up the otherwise sombre ruins of Errwood Hall, built by the Grimshawe family in 1830 but abandoned

▲ Stone bridges and moorland are common in the Goyt valley

when the estate was depopulated for the reservoir. The whole valley is noted for its rich vegetation.

GRINDLEFORD AND THE PADLEYS

MAP REF: 89SK2478

Grindleford Bridge spans the Derwent in a lovely setting between Eyam Moor and Froggatt Edge, at the apex of a triangle of roads. From there a minor route climbs west to curve round the lower slopes of Sir William Hill into Eyam, with a branch to Hucklow Edge. The B6001 runs north to Hathersage, and the B6521 north-east across the river and up through trees to Fox House Inn – named after a man called Fox.

From Grindleford station – actually in Upper Padley – along the B6521 is a track that leads beside the railway to the sparse ruins of Padley Manor House. Once the home of two devout Roman Catholic families, in 1588 the house witnessed the arrest of priests Nicholas Garlick and Robert Ludlam. Twelve days after being taken to Derby they, and another

▲ The River Goyt tumbling its way towards Errwood reservoir

a spacious market place that may once have been a green, a battlemented cruciform church with a dignified Perpendicular tower, a reasonably comprehensive range of shops and services, and a population of around 400. The actual parish is so vast that it was divided into four quarters – Upper, Nether, Middle and Town – the names of which still appear on maps.

Standing on the River Dove where its valley widens north of Beresford Dale, Hartington is a good centre from which to explore the Dove and Manifold valleys, and the central limestone uplands to the east. It offers good food at its several inns, good angling, pleasant walking and the opportunity for a peaceful half hour admiring the ducks on the village mere. The buildings are worthy of study too, being typical of the Peak and built of limestone – dressed or just plain rubble – with the more workable gritstone used for mullions, quoins and other architectural features.

Hartington Hall, a typical 17th-century Peakland manor house, was enlarged in the 19th century and now serves as a Youth Hostel. On rising ground east of the village, it numbers Bonnie Prince Charlie among its early guests. West of the village square Stilton is produced in the only cheese factory left in Derbyshire, where once there were a great many more.

The cheese, in a variety of plain, veined and flavoured forms, can be bought from a dairy shop near the village mere.

Above the river, 3 miles north at Pilsbury, are strange earthworks which may be the remains of a Norman motte-and-bailey castle built on the site of an Iron Age fort.

Haddon Hall, one of the finest medieval houses in England ▼

unfortunate, were hanged, drawn and quartered. The owner of the house, Thomas Fitzherbert, died in the Tower of London in 1591, and his brother John in Fleet Prison in 1598. The house was sold in 1657.

In 1933 the Roman Catholic Nottingham Diocese bought the original hall range and converted what had become a cowshed into a delightful chapel, to which a pilgrimage is made each July.

HADDON HALL
MAP REF: 93SK2366

On rising ground above the Wye and its meadows is the 'ideal' medieval manor house, a beautiful building to which the architecture of every century from the 12th to the 17th has contributed. After 1640 it stood empty because its owners, the Manners family – Earls and then Dukes of Rutland – made Belvoir Castle in Leicestershire their main residence. Then, this century, the father of the present Duke devoted most of his life to its scrupulously accurate restoration. It thus escaped any changes which may otherwise have resulted from the whims of fashion.

That it dodged military involvement also assisted its preservation – the turrets and battlements were never used.

The earliest work can be seen in the chapel, along with wall paintings and examples of work from all the other building periods. Sir John Manners added the impressive long gallery to the banquetting hall, kitchen, dining room, great chamber and 12ft perimeter wall built by the Vernon family. When it was finished in 1597 the building history of the house came to a complete and fitting end.

As to the story of the elopement of Dorothy Vernon and John Manners, neither the Dorothy Vernon bridge nor the bridge on which she allegedly joined her lover were there in her time. That, however, does not necessarily invalidate the tale, which – true or false – suits the Peakland environment.

HARTINGTON
MAP REF: 94SK1260

This gracious limestone village still has the atmosphere of the market town it became in 1203, featuring

THE REAL COST OF WATER

The deep gritstone dales and high rainfall of the Peak were a tempting prospect to the water engineers of the late 19th century, seeking to slake the ever-growing thirsts of the industrial cities in the surrounding lowlands.

Today, there are more than 50 reservoirs in the National Park, providing an entirely man-made element in the Peak District landscape. Despite their unnatural origins, they are often very popular with visitors and an enlightened attitude by the water authorities has seen many of them serving a dual purpose with numerous recreational opportunities.

The most famous series of reservoirs in the Peak are those which have flooded the Upper Derwent valley in the north-east of the National Park. The triple chain of Howden, Derwent and Ladybower reservoirs, usually simply known as 'the Dams', represent the largest area of water space in the park and have been dubbed the Peak's Lake District.

It was in 1899 that the Derwent Valley Water Board was set up, with the original purpose of constructing six reservoirs (later to be reduced to three) in the Derwent and Ashop valleys to serve the cities of Derby, Nottingham, Leicester and Sheffield with drinking water. The first two to be constructed were the Howden, highest up the valley in the shadow of Bleaklow, between 1901 and

▲ The Derwent Dam, one of three in the Derwent Valley, has a beauty of its own

1912, and the Derwent, which was built between 1902 and 1916.

To accomplish this massive project of civil engineering, a large workforce of navvies (so called because they first worked on the canal 'navigations') was needed. The DVWB resolved at an early stage 'to approve the erection of a village on a site near Birchinlee' which would house these nomadic workmen and their families over the 15 years of the contract.

The result was the extraordinary community of Birchinlee, popularly known as 'Tin Town' or 'Tin City' because of the green-painted, corrugated iron walls of the workmen's huts. Up to 1,000 people lived here in nearly 100 buildings, which included shops, a recreation hall, a school, a hospital, a 'canteen' (as the pub was known) and a police station.

Only a few scattered hill farms went under the waters of the Howden and Derwent reservoirs, and today nearly every trace of Tin Town is gone. However, when the larger Ladybower

reservoir was constructed between 1935 and 1943, the villages of Derwent and Ashopton had to be sacrificed under the rising waters. The villagers were rehoused in purpose-built accommodation at Yorkshire Bridge, just below the massive earthwork embankment of the dam, but many memories of their communities remain.

Among the buildings lost were stately Derwent Hall – dating from 1672 and a home of the Dukes of Norfolk, which had later become one of the first Youth Hostels in the Peak – and the Parish Church of St John and St James, Derwent.

Another stately mansion which was demolished by the water engineers for reasons of water purity was Errwood Hall, the Victorian home of the Grimshawe family in the Goyt valley.

Today, these water-filled valleys – often surrounded by dense coniferous forests – are a magnetic attraction to visitors. Traffic-management schemes, picnic areas, cycle hire and car parks have been provided to increase their enjoyment of these man-made landscapes.

Robin Hood's giant, Little John, was buried at Hathersage ▼

HATHERSAGE
MAP REF: 89SK2381

The A625 swoops down into Hathersage from the aptly-named Surprise View, where the land falls away suddenly to reveal an astonishing panorama of the hills around Kinder, across the valleys of the Noe and Derwent – whose waters meet on the village fringe.

Hathersage itself is large and prosperous, with hotels and shops lining a main road which drops to cross the Derwent and then enters the Hope valley by the junction with the B6001.

Less than 12 miles from Sheffield and linked to it by the Hope valley line from Manchester since 1894, Hathersage is a lively place with more than 60 local organisations.

Included is a thriving historical society which produces a useful village trail. This informs the visitor that for most of the 19th century Hathersage was a centre of the needle, pin and wire-drawing industry, with the tall chimneys of five mills 'belching out thick black smoke'. The industry, the smoke and the back-to-back houses vanished around the turn of the century, but four mills remain. One has been converted into luxury flats, and they all fulfil new uses.

The village's main tourist attraction – apart from the open-air swimming pool – is the grave of Little John in the churchyard, between yew trees 10ft apart. A 30in thigh-bone exhumed here in 1784 was subsequently stolen. The

▲ Hathersage nestles in the green Vale of Hope

church, much restored by Butterfield in 1852, contains Eyre monuments which may have given Charlotte Brontë the surname for her heroine in *Jane Eyre*. The Eyres reputedly owned seven houses around Hathersage, among them North Lees, which was bought by the Peak Park Board in 1971. This Elizabethan tower house is now the nucleus of a farm, and also provides holiday accommodation. Parts of its 1,200-acre estate are open to the public.

HAYFIELD
MAP REF: 87SK0387

Where the boisterous little River Sett bustles down from the Kinder massif on to relatively level ground, the tall gritstone buildings of Hayfield snuggle compactly along its narrow valley. The A624 road tumbles down from the 1,000ft contour line at Chinley Head to cut through the village on a new bypass, and then climbs

▼ Hayfield's Pack Horse Inn

sharply to reach 1,000ft again at attractive Hollingworth Head.

Some 1½ miles beyond Little Hayfield – dominated by Clough Mill in the west and Park Hall, whose nearest eastward neighbour is nearly 20 miles away on the other side of Kinder Scout – is a left turn on to the Charlesworth road, just short of the Grouse Inn. This leads along Monks Road – named after the monks of Basingwerk Abbey in Flint, who owned land hereabouts from the 12th to the 16th century – to Coombes Edge and a remarkable view of two Englands. All around is some of the wildest, emptiest land in the country, while below is the vast sprawl of matchbox buildings in Greater Manchester. The scene could have been tailor-made for artist, L S Lowry, who lived on the edge of that uninspiring area at Mottram-in-Longdendale.

Hayfield has a foot in both Englands, with an economy based on wool, water and walking. First came the sheep, whose wool was woven on frames in tall attics – then in even taller mills powered by the River Sett. Wool gave way to cotton, which was itself displaced by calico printing, and paper making in the 1860s. Now there is just one paper mill, but paint is manufactured in Clough Mill at Little Hayfield. Sheep are still reared, and Hayfield remains the last refreshment stop for walkers tackling Edale Moor and Kinder Scout from the west – just as it was when the Pack Horse Inn was built in 1577 to cater for 'jaggers' (teamsmen) and their trains of 20 or 30 packhorses.

An incongruously urban subway funnels pedestrians under the bypass to Hayfield station, now the start of the 2½-mile Sett Valley Trail for horse riders and walkers. The going along this old track is good and level.

HOLME
MAP REF: 83SE1006

Below the 1,900ft summit of Holme Moss, the infant River Holme tumbles into West Yorkshire and out of the National Park beyond Holme village, where the Huddersfield buses turn and the wilderness ends. The A6024 road from Longdendale, often blocked by winter snow, descends alongside.

At 1,000ft, Holme is the highest and oldest settlement in the Holme valley, the only one mentioned in the *Domesday* survey. Much later it became involved in the woollen trade, which accounts for its tall houses of three and sometimes four storeys. The occupants of these gritstone, mullion-windowed cottages needed all available light in upper rooms, where they wove their cloth.

One ultra-modern house has no storeys above ground, however. This is the aptly-named 'Underhill', built into the hillside by the architect Arthur Quarmby as his family home. His lawn is also his roof.

Down the lane leading to Digley reservoir the walls have holes to hold tenter hooks for stretching drying cloth. Digley is one of the numerous attractive reservoirs in the valley with picnic areas.

▲ *Last of the Summer Wine* featured Nora Batty's House at Holmfirth

HOLMFIRTH
MAP REF: 83SE1408

Having narrowly missed becoming Britain's 'Hollywood', Holmfirth has achieved fame as the centre of *Last of the Summer Wine* country, where visitors who flock to the TV home of Foggy, Cleggy and Compo can follow in their footsteps by horse and trap provided by Nora Batty's Tours.

The village has been involved with the entertainment industry much longer than that, however, and was making pictures in 1870 when James Bamforth began producing magic lantern slides by photographing live models against his own hand-painted backcloths. He turned the slides into picture postcards as a successful sideline, and later in around 1908 progressed to movies. By then he was bringing professional players to Holmfirth by special trains to make films in the Holme valley, but war ended production for good and Hollywood became dominant. The resourceful Bamforth concentrated then on comic postcards, inventing the seaside landlady and the stout female in a bathing costume whose grand daughters adorn postcards produced today by the family's modern generation.

The River Holme is a mere 8 miles long from its source at the foot of Holme Moss, below the 725ft mast of the BBC transmitter, to the River Colne at Huddersfield. It looks placid as it flows through the heart of Holmfirth, but three times in two centuries it has caused devastating floods with loss of life. Some 81 souls were drowned in the terrible disaster of 1852 when nearby Bilberry dam burst.

Holy Trinity Church was rebuilt after the 1777 flood as a most attractive Georgian 'preaching box', with galleries on three sides and painted now in blue and white after the style of the better-known Shobbden Church in Herefordshire.

If the Sunday before Whitsun is wet, the 'Holmfirth Sing' is held in the church; if fine, it is held in Victoria Park. This community singing of hymns and *Messiah* selections, an annual event since 1882, grew from the Holmfirth Festival founded in 1726.

Another annual event, the Harden Moss Sheepdog Trials, is held on two days in June on the moors off the A635.

HOPE
MAP REF: 88SK1783

Historically, this village was first mentioned in 926, when King Athelstan won a battle nearby. By 1068 its parish embraced two-thirds of the Royal Forest of the High Peak, including Buxton, Tideswell and Chapel-en-le-Frith, and a century ago it was still one of the largest in the country.

Of the original church mentioned in the *Domesday* survey, only the Norman font – recovered from the vicarage garden – remains. The present building, with its conspicuous, stumpy broach tower, dates mainly from 1200 and was reroofed in stainless steel during the 1970s. The fine pulpit of 1652 bears the name of Thomas Bocking – vicar, schoolmaster and Royalist – whose chair in the north aisle bears a Latin inscription translatable as 'You cannot make a

scholar out of a block of wood'. His 1599 'Breeches' Bible is exhibited nearby. Two foliated 13th-century cross slabs with incised foresters' arms are memorials to Royal Forest officials.

The nearby Woodruffe Arms commemorates a local family who may once have held the office of wood reeve, and the 'Old Hall Hotel' was built in the early 17th century as a manor house for the Balguy family. They also built houses at Derwent and Aston, a centreless hamlet strung out along narrow lanes on the slopes of Win Hill to the east. In 1715 Hope obtained a charter for a market which is still held weekly. Nearly opposite the Old Hall is Daggers House (with cross-daggers engraved above the door), which was built in the 18th century as the Cross Daggers Inn. Along the Pin Dale road are the remains of a pinfold, where stray beasts were at one time impounded.

Although it has at least a dozen establishments offering bed and breakfast, Hope is perhaps less geared to tourism than neighbouring Castleton and Edale. However, it is undisputedly the educational centre for the valley, with its fine college opened in 1958.

ILAM AND THE MANIFOLD VALLEY
MAP REF: 94SK1350

After rising close together on Axe Edge and following almost parallel courses, the Dove and Manifold merge near Ilam, a handsome estate village in romantic surroundings. Shipping magnate Jesse Watts Russell employed John Shaw to rebuild Ilam Hall in a battlemented Gothic style, and to rebuild the whole village in the cottage *ornée* fashion. The tile-hanging and barge-boarded gables are unusual in the Peak – as too is the 30ft imitation Eleanor Cross which he raised in memory of his first wife. In 1855 Gilbert Scott over-restored the ancient, saddleback-towered church, which

The lofty crag of Thor's Cave yawns over the Manifold valley ▶

was already dominated by Chantrey's overlarge monument to Russell's father-in-law, David Watts. Fortunately, he left undisturbed the shrine of St Bertelin (or Bertram), a late-Saxon saint.

When demolition of the hall began in 1934, Sir Robert McDougall bought what was left – along with parts of both the Dove and Manifold valleys – and gave them to the National Trust. The hall is leased to the Youth Hostel Association. William Congreve wrote his bawdy play *The Old Bachelor*, and Dr Johnson received his inspiration for *Rasselas*, in the hall grounds.

The Manifold has many of the Dove's attributes. Its valley is only marginally less beautiful and usually decidedly less crowded – even though it has a good footpath along the track of the old Leek and Manifold Light Railway (1904–34).

The only part of the valley below Hulme End that is accessible to motorists is the short section between the former Redhurst Halt and Butterton station. Below Beeston Tor is a deserted village site and there is what may have been a Romano-British settlement near the ruins of Throwley Hall.

The Manifold villages are sited high above the gorge, and the entrance to Butterton is through an unusually long ford. Both Butterton and Grindon have architecturally uninspiring churches with prominent spires. The one at Grindon, on the edge of a common, contains a memorial to six RAF men who died when their aircraft crashed while 'bringing relief to the stricken villages during the great blizzard of 1947'. Two press photographers died with them shortly after parachuting food and supplies to the people of Wetton, Onecote, Butterton and Grindon.

In Wetton church is the grave of Samuel Carrington – village schoolmaster who, with Thomas Bateman of Middleton-by-Youlgreave, excavated a sizeable Romano-British settlement at Borough Fields and at Long Low. They discovered two round, late-Neolithic cairns uniquely linked by a contemporary stone bank, and half a mile south-west of the village at Thor's Cave they found evidence of occupation in the Iron Age and Romano-British times. The cave impressively overlooks the east bank of the Manifold.

Water is a pleasing contrast to woodland at Ilam Hall ▶

▲ Two Saxon stone crosses can be seen in the churchyard at Ilam

Like the Manifold, the Hamps vanishes into its limestone bed on its course through charming, empty country. The nearest village, Waterfall, lies 2 miles west and is as pretty as its name, as is the tiny satellite of Back o' th' Brook.

LEEK
MAP REF: 80SJ9856

Cobbles, mills and sombre stone buildings give 'the Capital of the Moorlands' the forbidding appearance of a Lancashire cotton town that has somehow slipped into Staffordshire. However, there is more to this hillside town than that, including a charming little cobbled market place. The interesting church displays a variety of styles, with much stained glass by Morris & Co. It has two late-Saxon crosses in its churchyard. Leek's School of Needlework was founded by Elizabeth Wardle – later Lady Wardle – around 1870, and there is a James Brindley water mill which opens at weekends and on bank holidays.

A museum, library and art school are housed in the Nicholson Institute, a pleasing building of 1884 by the local architect William Sugden. This is half hidden behind the town's finest house, 17th-century Greystones.

Leek's mills produced mainly silk goods and some cotton, hence the Leek Embroidery Society and its Bayeux Tapestry replica now housed in Reading Museum. The mills are used for dyeing, finishing and food-processing purposes.

The wild and lovely moorland receives fewer visitors than it deserves. Only 2 miles south is the North Staffordshire Steam Railway Centre at Cheddleton station, which runs a small museum. Close by on the other side of the Churnet, where the re-opened Caldon Canal reaches the valley, are the restored buildings of the Cheddleton Flint Mill. From around 1800 flint was ground here for use in china manufacture.

South from Cheddleton, the Churnet valley is so steep-sided and thickly wooded that it is inaccessible in places, even to walkers. Remains of industry are almost buried under vegetation, as at Consall Ironworks, but horse-drawn narrow boats from Froghall Wharf on Thursdays, Sundays and some Saturdays offer an enjoyable means of exploration.

In 1975 the National Park Board bought the 975-acre Roaches Estate, north-east of Leek, to ensure its 'maximum public benefit in perpetuity'. Wonderful walking is available along the 2-mile serrated edge of this astonishing gritstone outcrop, with rock climbing, too, and superb views from 1,600ft of similar height ranges in all directions. Conical Hen Cloud rises to the south-east.

THE DELIGHTFUL DALES

John Ruskin, the 19th-century art critic and early conservationist, was quite definite in his views of the respective merits of dale and moorland scenery in the Peak. 'The whole gift of the country is in its glens,' he claimed. 'The wide acreage of field or moor above is wholly without interest; it is only in the clefts of it, and the dingles, that the traveller finds his joy.'

Most modern visitors would probably not be quite so dismissive of the rolling limestone plateau of the White Peak, with its fascinating relics from prehistory and its charming villages – but it is still the dales which dissect the plateau with their precipitous crags, verdant woodlands and nature reserves which provide the real scenic gems of the White Peak.

Geologists believe the dales were formed in the Carboniferous limestone at the end of the last Ice Age, when tremendous volumes of freezing melt water flowed out from the shrinking glaciers and snowfields, cutting through the rock like a knife through butter. Limestone, formed from the fossilised skeletons of sea-creatures some 330 million years ago, is a heavily jointed rock that can be dissolved by rainwater.

This means that many of the White Peak dales are now dry, or only occasionally have a river flowing through them, as the water dives underground through swallet, swallow, or 'shakeholes'. Examples of this are the dramatic dry gorges of The Winnats and Cave Dale, near Castleton, and the disappearing rivers of the Manifold, Hamps, Bradford and Lathkill farther south.

What happens to the water when it disappears underground? The answer is that it creates yet another, usually unseen landscape of caves and caverns, which honeycomb the White Peak.

The 'hollow country' where the limestone and the gritstone, the White and Dark Peaks, meet around Castleton is where modern visitors can be introduced to the Peak's 'underground'. Well-lit show caves like Treak Cliff, Blue John, Speedwell and Bagshawe, at neighbouring Bradwell, attract thousands of visitors every year. The yawning void of Peak Cavern, beneath the ruins of Peveril Castle, is the largest cave entrance in Britain, and formerly housed a whole community of rope-makers. The soot from the chimneys of this subterranean village can still be seen in the cavern roof.

Thor's Cave, above the Manifold valley near Wetton, is one of many Peakland caves which have revealed evidence of occupation by prehistoric man.

MAP REF: 88SK1675

Litton, clean-lined and compact, stands at almost 1,000ft on limestone uplands above the Wye. Its main street, which has a triangular green at its western end and a wide strip of green down both sides, is a good place to study the vernacular architecture of the Peak. Many of the houses have date-stones – the earliest being

▲ Litton has limestone buildings and small, stone-walled fields of ancient pattern

1639 – but the average is about a century later, towards the end of the period that Professor W G Hoskins called 'the Great Rebuilding'. It was a boom time in the local lead industry, too, which may explain the comparative lavishness of Clergy House (1723) and Hammerton House (1768). The combined church, school and library was given by Canon Samuel Andrews – vicar of Tideswell (then including Litton) – in 1865, and a modern church was built in 1929. Litton retains close affinities with Tideswell, even to dressing its well on the same day – the Saturday which falls closest to St John the Baptist's Day (24 June).

Cressbrook clings precariously to the lower slopes of the hillside above the Wye, its cottages terraced among ash woods. At the

Thor's Cave, one of several remarkable caves in the Manifold valley, is 60ft wide ▼

lowest level is a row that was formerly the apprentice house, where pauper apprentices from London and elsewhere lived during the short intervals between their long working days in Cressbrook Mill. They were well treated under William Newton, a local, self-made business man and poet. Those at Litton Mill told a different story, as related by one Robert Blincoe, who spent the worst years of his life there shortly after 1800.

Cressbrook Mill is a handsome

building of 1815, partly used but in urgent need of restoration. The stretch of the Wye between the mills is known as Water-Cum-Jolly Dale. Cressbrook Dale is a pretty, thickly-wooded tributary valley running north from Monsal Dale.

LONGNOR

MAP REF: 91SK0965

In lonely moorland country on the River Manifold, Longnor still has something of the appearance and air of the market town it once was. At the upper end of a small, sloping and cobbled market place is a market house that was built in 1873, when Longnor was a prosperous farming community. A scale of market charges is posted on a board outside. The prosperity faded, however, as agricultural depression set in. The coaching age had already gone, the roads radiating from Longnor and its

coaching inns were empty and the railway never arrived to fill the gap. Longnor's population declined from 561 in 1861 to 364 in 1981, with corresponding falls in most villages on this west side of the Peak.

Happily, the decline has been arrested in recent years. The village became a conservation area in 1977 and has been the subject of much good restoration by the National Park Authority. New workshops have been added in an 'integrated rural development' experiment. Craftsmen work in the market house, and a small industrial estate has been established on the outskirts.

Longnor is an excellent touring centre. North is a remarkable array of conical hills near the headwaters of the Dove, providing some of the Peak District's few genuine peaks. High Wheeldon (1,383ft) was given to the nation as a memorial to Derbyshire and Staffordshire men killed in World War II, then transferred to the National Trust. At its foot was a packhorse route that crossed the Dove at Crowdecote. The Quiet Woman Inn in the long, quarrying village of Earl Sterndale – tucked away between High Wheeldon and Parkhouse – shows a headless woman on its sign. Earl Sterndale church dates from 1952. Its predecessor was destroyed by a bomb in January 1941.

South-west of Longnor, the long, curving bulk of Morridge (Moor Edge) forms the natural western boundary of the National Park. The road along it, probably an ancient ridgeway, offers splendid views and leads at its northern end to the lonely Mermaid Inn – with its legend of a mermaid enticing strangers into the nearby Black Mere (or Mermaid Pool). There is also an apparently true story of a murder taking place here, while another speaks of an attempted killing.

LONGSHAW

MAP REF: 89SK2678

Over 1,500 acres of open moorland and woodland comprise the lovely Longshaw Estate, owned by the National Trust and designated a country park. At its heart is a former shooting lodge of the Dukes of Rutland.

Through the area – which extends from Fox House Inn to below Surprise View and includes Padley Wood – flows the Burbage Brook on its way south to the Derwent. Not far from its source north of the A625 road it runs below Carl Wark, a mysterious fortification on the edge of a plateau. Recent research suggests that it may date from considerably later than the various Iron Age forts in the Peak. On opposite sides of the brook at Lawrence Field and Sheffield Plantation are remnants of early village settlements.

South of the main road, relics of ancient natural woodland may have survived in parts of Padley Wood where the ground was too steep, rough and rocky for grazing sheep.

On the open moorland weathering has carved outcropping gritstone into strange and contorted shapes, such as Toad's Mouth Rock, near the road. The numerous millstones scattered around, especially near Millstone Edge, were probably abandoned when the trade in local stones collapsed. The industry declined gradually after the introduction of roller mills in 1862. Sheep dog trials are held at Longshaw in early September.

▼ Still waters at Longshaw Estate

▲ Fishing at Ridgegate reservoir in Macclesfield Forest. A tiny hamlet with a small chapel is hidden by the trees

LONGSTONE
MAP REF: 92SK2071

Great Longstone, which is the larger of the two Longstones, is an attractive, stone-built village stretching out from a small green and approached from the west along an avenue of elms. The Hall – a good, unfussy building of 1747 – is, surprisingly, of brick. This was presumably a piece of one-upmanship in an area abounding with building stone.

Little Longstone is strung out along the road a mile to the west. It is built wholly of stone, including the late 17th-century manor house and another of 1575.

A farther half a mile to the west, at the end of the road, the ground suddenly falls away to give a stunning view of the River Wye as it runs through Monsal Dale. The great stone Monsal viaduct dominates the left foreground, beyond which rises Fin Cop with traces of an Iron Age fort at its summit.

Two miles east of Great Longstone is the little village of Hassop, dominated by the Roman Catholic Church of All Saints. It was built between 1816 and 1818 for the Eyre family of Hassop Hall, an early 17th-century house enlarged in 1830 and now an hotel – with a lead-mine shaft in its cellar. Hassop station, 2 miles south of the village, was built in 1863 by Edward Walters to serve the Duke of Devonshire, rather than Hassop itself. It is now a bookshop along the route of the Monsal Trail, which continues from here over Monsal viaduct.

Over all broods Longstone Edge (1,300ft), which affords good views and is the site of several tumuli. Fluorspar working has caused some damage, though limited restoration has also taken place in recent years.

The south front of lovely Lyme Park, seen across the lake. It has 1,300 acres of grounds ▼

LYME PARK
MAP REF: 86SJ9682

When Sir Piers Legh married Margaret Danyers in 1388 he became the owner of Lyme Hanley in the Forest of Macclesfield, given in 1346 to her father Sir Thomas Danyers for services to Edward III in battle at Caen. Exactly 600 years later, Richard Legh, 3rd Lord Newton, gave Lyme Park to the National Trust – for whom it is administered as a country park by Stockport Borough Council.

The 7th of 11 Sir Piers Leghs greatly enlarged an existing house in around 1570, and it is this Elizabethan work that forms the core of the present building. Little of it is visible from the outside, except on the north (entrance) front. Even there the substitution of later sash windows and the addition of end bays makes the 16th-century work less obvious.

Around this early house, to which a few piecemeal alterations had already been made, the Venetian architect Giacomo Leoni built a vast Palladian mansion with an impressive Ionic portico rising to three storeys on the south front facing the lake. Lewis Wyatt made other additions early in the 19th century, and although the magnificent limewood carvings in the saloon are attributed by family tradition to Grinling Gibbons, much of the interior work was by local craftsmen.

The entrance to Lyme Park – off the A6 at Disley – is at the approach to suburban Stockport, but the estate lies wholly in the National Park and its deer park stretches back on to the moors.

MACCLESFIELD
MAP REF: 80SJ9273

An ancient market town on the lower, western slopes of the Pennines, Macclesfield has little to show from its earliest history, but the town turned in 1756 to the silk industry, gradually replacing Derby as the national centre of the trade. The last handloom weaver retired in 1981 when the firm of Cartwright & Sheldon closed down, but Paradise Mill – in which it was housed – has re-opened as a working museum. It is within five minutes' walk of the Macclesfield Silk Museum and Heritage Centre in Roe Street.

East of the town centre the A537 Buxton road climbs steadily on to the moors, passing at 750ft Eddisbury Park Field – 16 acres of park-like meadow owned by the National Trust and which affords marvellous views across the Cheshire Plain.

The wild country south of the A537, from Walker Barn on the National Park boundary to the county boundary beyond the Cat and Fiddle Inn, once lay within medieval Macclesfield Forest. Now somewhat reduced in size, it survives as a managed coniferous forest containing a tiny chapel where a traditional rush-bearing ceremony is held in August. The Cat and Fiddle Inn, south of Shining Tor (1,834ft) was built in 1820 to catch the passing coach trade.

MATLOCK
MAP REF: 93SK3060

There are eight Matlocks with eight other hamlets making up a sizeable town which most people simply think of as Matlock. The oldest part is Old Matlock, where an 18th-century rectory can be found next to Wheatsheaf Farm of 1681, which has the only mullioned and transomed windows in the place. Thermal water was discovered here in 1698, and Matlock Bath was born as a spa of sorts. However, it was handicapped by having only 'a base, stony, mountainous road to it and no good accommodation when you are there'. Things have changed!

The building of the Old Bath Hotel in the 1730s and the opening of what is now the A6 through Scarthin Nick in 1818, overcame such problems, and Matlock Bath achieved popularity. This was especially so with day trippers, who came first by canal to Cromford Wharf and then by train to Joseph Paxton's Swiss-chalet railway station (now the Derbyshire Wildlife Trust's 'Whistlestop Centre'), driving the long-stay visitor up the road to Smedley's Hydro (1853). For the next century this up-market hotel-cum-health farm dominated the town – as it does still as the headquarters of the Derbyshire County Council.

John Smedley, a dogmatic and eccentric industrialist who ran the Hydro (and Matlock), built himself the fairy-tale Riber Castle above the town. Standing in the grounds of Riber Wildlife Park, it is shortly to be redeveloped as a hotel.

Matlock Bath is still the lively end of town, with lots happening in and around the Pavilion by the Derwent. There is also a good lead-mining museum and a tourist information centre. The whole town is worth seeing for the beauty of its setting in a deep

High on a hill above Matlock, 19th-century Riber Castle dominates the town ▼

▲ Cable cars now take tourists up the Heights of Abraham

gorge, best viewed from the cable cars which shuttle backwards and forwards high above. Architecturally, this is a Victorian town, in a fascinating area where there are caves in the hillsides – mostly old lead mines, possibly Roman – unexpected gardens on hilltops and excellent places for walking within easy reach.

MELTHAM

MAP REF: 83SE0910

Mills and moors dominate Meltham. The Victorian mills are massive, impressive and perhaps oppressive, while the moors lie at the end of every twisting, hilly street of this distinctively Pennine (rather than Peakland) woollen town. In both atmosphere and geography it is not far from J B Priestley's 'Bruddersford'.

The Carlile Institute of 1890 – including the public library – and the adjacent, slightly forbidding town hall are the most important public buildings in the main street. They are, however, less imposing than the great mill complex, with its tall red-brick building in the steep little valley below. Above – because everything in Meltham is either above or below – is what was originally an octagonal school building, 'built by subscription in 1823'. A later extension at the rear masks the shape from that side.

South-west of Meltham a minor road climbs to 1,640ft and joins the A635 for the crossing of Saddleworth Moor into Lancashire.

▲ The tiny village of Miller's Dale has old houses and textile mills

MILLER'S DALE
MAP REF: 92SK1373

This little settlement squeezed itself awkwardly into the narrow valley of the Wye – below the Midland railway junction for Buxton on the main St Pancras-to-Manchester line – in the 1860s, providing housing for rail men and workers in various industries that had followed in the wake of the railway.

All these and the station, which also served as the village post office, have gone. The viaduct now carries the National Park's Monsal Trail footpath along the former railway track above the valley. The limeworks above the railway were spectacularly blown up in 1971, and their quarry is now a nature reserve. Four stone lime kilns dating from 1878 have been stabilised and are open to the public.

The hamlet takes its name from one of the best known of several beautiful dales accessible along the Wye to walkers. South of Buxton the A6 twists and turns alongside the river through Ashwood Dale, and is crossed in many places by the Midland railway line. Where the road leaves the river at the foot of Topley Pike the approach to Wye Dale is marred by a large quarry. Farther along there is the giant Tunstead Quarry – the largest in Europe and a producer of exceptionally pure limestone – which sprawls along Great Rocks Dale, a tributary valley.

From there to its confluence with the Derwent at Rowsley, however, the Wye is a gloriously clear and lovely river. The riverside path wanders through Chee, Miller's and Monsal Dales, providing some 6 miles of delightful walking. Chee Dale has a 50-acre nature reserve which includes Chee Tor, a prominent 300ft cliff with an exposed rock face, popular with climbers, above the river.

MONYASH
MAP REF: 92SK1566

A bed of clay about 100yds square probably explains why Monyash is isolated in a slight bowl some 1,000ft up on the limestone uplands. For at the junction of the clay and limestone rose 23 springs which were retained in five natural meres on the impervious deposits. Fere Mere, the sole survivor but

EARLY TOURISTS

Despite its modern popularity, the Peak District received a very bad press at the hands of its earliest tourists. For instance, the 16th-century poet, Michael Drayton, described it as: 'A withered bedlam long, with bleared, waterish eyes; With many a bleak storm dimmed, which often to the skies; She cast, and oft to th' earth bowed down her aged head; Her meagre, wrinkled face being sullied still with lead.'

Probably the first tourist guidebook to the Peak was written in long-winded Latin verse by Thomas Hobbes, the philosopher and tutor to the Cavendishes at Chatsworth. His De Mirabilibus Pecci: Concerning the Wonders of the Peak in Darby-shire published in 1636, listed seven 'wonders' which he had visited during a two-day ride.

They were: Aedes, Mons, Barathrum, binus Fons, Antraque bina – or a house (Chatsworth); a mountain (Mam Tor); a chasm (Eldon Hole); two fountains (St Ann's Well in Buxton and the Ebbing and Flowing Well at Barmoor); and two caves (Poole's Cavern in Buxton and Peak Cavern, Castleton).

These wonders were later rehashed by Charles Cotton, squire of Beresford Hall in Dovedale and co-author with Izaac Walton of The Compleat Angler. However, even Cotton condemned Dovedale as 'this craggy, ill-contrived nook', while praising its trout-filled waters as 'the princess of rivers'.

The tour of the Seven Wonders of the Peak became an accepted and fashionable itinerary to those early visitors, including the redoubtable daughter of a Roundhead colonel, Celia Fiennes, who rode side-saddle through England in 1697. She wrote: 'All Derbyshire is full of steep hills, and nothing but the peakes of hills as thick as one by another is seen in most of the County which are very steepe which makes travelling tedious, and the miles long, you see neither hedge not tree but only low drye stone walls round some ground, else its only hills and dales as thick as you can imagine'.

Edward Browne, Norfolk-born son of Sir Thomas Browne, in his Journal of a Tour in Derbyshire (1662) found it a 'strange, mountainous, misty, moorish, rocky, wild country', while the cynical journalist and author, Daniel Defoe, was even more scathing of this 'howling wilderness'. 'This, perhaps, is the most desolate, wild and abandoned country in all England', he suggested in his Tour Through the Whole Island of Great Britain (1726) – adding that he found the inhabitants 'a rude boorish kind of people'. He poured scorn on the 'Wonders' of Hobbes and Cotton, dismissing all but Eldon Hole and Chatsworth, 'one a wonder of nature, the other of art'.

Later visitors, like Lord Byron and John Ruskin, helped to develop the national taste for wild scenery. Byron claimed: 'there are things in Derbyshire as noble as in Greece or Switzerland', while Ruskin called the county 'a lovely child's alphabet; an alluring first lesson in all that is admirable'.

▼ Early tourists in the Peak Cavern

once the village's source of drinking water, stands within a stone enclosure built to deter cattle and close to the central cross-roads. Nearby is a well that is dressed annually, probably as a thanksgiving for the water.

The market cross on the green has a medieval base and is the only indication – apart, perhaps, from the size of the church – that Monyash received a charter for a market in 1340. This plugged a 'trade gap' between Hartington and Bakewell. A village market is now held on the green on the two summer bank holidays.

A village so isolated had to be self-supporting, and the industries of Monyash have included a flint-tool 'factory' in prehistoric times, candle making, rope making, building meres for the farms around (redundant and fast disappearing since the belated arrival of piped water on these uplands), quarrying and lead mining – as evidenced by the mine hillocks littering the local fields. The 17th-century Bull's Head, now quaintly renamed the Hobbit, is the sole survivor of five village pubs.

Monyash was a Quaker stronghold in the late 18th century, but the movement has faded here, like the industries. The Barmote Court still meets occasionally, however, to adjudicate in mineral disputes occurring in the immediate area.

Among many excellent walks around the village, the most popular is down the River Lathkill, which in winter rises in a cave south-east of the village just beyond the disused Ricklow Quarry. This one-time source of Ashford Marble (see page 34) is below Parson Tor, where a Monyash vicar fell to his death in 1776. In dry spells the river may rise much lower down its bed, near Over Haddon.

NEW MILLS
MAP REF: 86SK0085

The new mill (just one) was built on the River Sett for grinding corn, around 1750, in the hamlet of Ollerset – one of several tiny settlements sited between Kinder Scout and the Goyt and once known collectively as Bowden Middlecale.

Ollerset and neighbouring Beard, Thornsett and Whittle were grouped together as a single township that came to be known as New Mills, which was adopted as the official name of a parish formed in 1884. Soon there developed a town dominated by new cotton mills, some of which have survived, with their chimneys – along with spiky churches, solid Nonconformist chapels and rows of dark gritstone cottages which give the place its Lowry look. What really catches the eye is the deep gorge of the Goyt winding through the town centre, the splendid array of stone viaducts and bridges which span it, and the splendour of the brooding hills all around.

Among those hills to the north lies the tiny but beautiful hamlet of Rowarth. A footpath running north from there passes in less than a mile near a pair of round pillars set in a rock. Maps call them Robin Hood's Picking Rods, and tradition has it that they were used for bending and stringing bows. No better suggestion has been forthcoming, but they may have had connections with the Basingwerk Abbey monks, for Monks Road is fairly near.

For those who prefer walking on the level, New Mills is at the western end of the Sett Valley Trail from Hayfield, and also at the end of the river which joins the Goyt here.

Close to the confluence at the entrance to The Torrs is a new heritage information centre, which has displays showing the history and development of the town.

OVER HADDON
MAP REF: 92SK2066

The alphabetical accident which places Over Haddon next to New Mills serves to emphasise the enormous variety of Peak scenery, because no two places could provide a greater contrast. Over Haddon seems to float among the clouds when seen from the terraced garden of Haddon Hall, in the manor of Nether Haddon, and is a typical rural village of the limestone plateau. Its site at 800ft above sea level gives excellent views – especially south across Lathkill Dale to the tower of Youlgreave Church and far across the moors of Harthill and Gratton beyond.

Yet Over Haddon has an industrial past, with the relics of its lead mines still visible in the dale. The ruins of Mandale Mine's pumping house are down there among the thick foliage. So too is the leat (channel) which took water from a weir to turn the wheels of the Mandale and the Lathkill Dale mines, and the pillars of an aqueduct which carried it across the river. Close by are the remains of Carter's corn mill, but there is no trace – and never was – of the 'gold' which nearly turned Over Haddon into a mini-Klondike in the 1850s. It turned out to be iron pyrites, also known as fools' gold.

Facing Over Haddon on the opposite rim of the dale is Meadow Place Grange, one of a number of local monastic farms that were once at the heart of immense sheep ranches. John Bright, of 19th-century Anti-Corn League fame, spent his honeymoon at One Ash Grange in a tributary valley called Cales Dale, higher upstream. One Ash belonged to the Cistercian house of Roche Abbey in Yorkshire.

In very dry weather the River Lathkill emerges from a long way down its true course, often necessitating the rescue of fish from the upper reaches. Repairs by Peak Park Conservation volunteers have been carried out on the bed and banks of the river to prevent this.

Downstream from Over Haddon, the Nature Conservancy Council in 1972 established the Peak's first National Nature Reserve, in mainly ash and elm woodland. It features a variety of shrubs, including the rare mezereon.

▼ The River Lathkill, seen from Conksbury Bridge at Over Haddon

PARWICH
MAP REF: 95SK1854

A mile inside the south-eastern corner of the Peak Park is Parwich, which sits pleasantly around and above a green in an area where the limestone uplands drop to the valley of Bradbourne Brook. Parwich Hall, standing commandingly above the village and digging its back into a sharply rising hillside, is conspicuous for being of brick in a mainly stone-built village. As it was completed in 1747 – the same year as similarly brick-built Great Longstone Hall – suspicions of rivalry must be aroused.

On Parwich Moor above the village are more than 70 embanked capped at about 1,200ft by a few dying beech trees around the remains of several Neolithic chambered tombs.

From Minninglow car park, on the High Peak Trail, runs the 4-mile circular Roystone Grange Archaeological Trail. Using the former railway track, fields and farm tracks, this passes the remains of a medieval farm – of which the dairy has been excavated – plus a 'fossil' Roman field system, traces of a Roman manor house and farm buildings, and evidence of later quarrying and mining. Trail booklets are available from information centres and elsewhere, but shops in the immediate area are rarer than ancient remains.

▲ In the shadow of a great hill, the church and neat stone houses of Parwich can be found clustered around a green

circles of varying sizes and unknown function. They probably date from the Bronze Age but do not seem to be funerary.

Parwich Church is Victorian but retains from an earlier building a fine Norman tympanum over the north doorway. Alsop en le Dale lies 3 miles west and is at the start of various footpaths leading to Milldale, at the northern end of Dovedale. Its small church has a Norman nave and an interesting south doorway of that period. Ballidon, one mile east of Parwich, has an even smaller chapel sited in a field. This has much early Norman work that was regrettably over-restored in 1882. It must have served the deserted medieval village, traces of which exist in the surrounding fields. The tiny village itself is completely overwhelmed by a large quarry and its attendant works.

A minor road from Parwich heads north to Pikehall, an agricultural hamlet which may have been more important in coaching days. The road passes close to Minninglow,

PEAK FOREST
MAP REF: 87SK1179

Nothing could be more misleading than the name of this village, which shelters in a dip on the A623 road. Apart from a healthy clump of trees acting as a wind-break around the church, the landscape is almost bare. It seems to have been that way for a long time, for this part of the High Peak Forest was called *Campagna* – meaning 'open country' – and probably had few trees even before lead smelting and the Civil War took their toll.

Forest courts were held here in Chamber Farm, which was rebuilt in the 18th century, and were conducted by the Steward of the Forest with not fewer than 20 foresters. They ensured that forest laws were enforced justly and without undue harshness.

The church given by the 7th Duke of Devonshire in 1877 has retained the unusual dedication to King Charles the Martyr of its more interesting predecessor, which was built by Christian, Countess of Devonshire in 1657. She intended it as a private chapel within the royal forest and outside the jurisdiction of a bishop. It was also outside the law in that it was erected during a Commonwealth ban on church-building. The incumbent – in full, 'the Principal Officer and Judge in Spiritualities in the Peculiar Court of Peak Forest' – took advantage of his unusual position to make money from marriages. These he conducted without question at any time of day or night. Peak Forest was a Peakland equivalent of Gretna Green until Lord Hardwicke's Marriage Act of 1753 restricted marriage services to daylight hours only. Even then, clandestine marriages continued until 1804.

About a mile north of Peak Forest is Eldon Hole, the so-called 'Bottomless Pit' and one of the traditional Seven Wonders of the Peak. It is actually 200ft deep, and one of the few good-sized pot holes in the National Park. Another is 495ft Giant's Hole, situated on the other side of Eldon near the foot of Rushup Edge.

PENISTONE
MAP REF: 85SE2403

Quietly flows the Don past – rather than through – Penistone before entering the industrial sprawl of Sheffield, and the market town itself stands handsomely above the river in two shades of gritstone. Its mainly 14th-century, battlemented church appears particularly sombre from without – probably the result of centuries of smoke pollution, much reduced in recent years – but not even a coating of soot can hide its intrinsic attractiveness.

Between the church in its pleasant churchyard at the top of the town, and the long main street curving gently down under one of many railway bridges before dropping into the valley, stands a former market hall in the classical style – now used for various other purposes.

Penistone is a musical town – as Pennine towns tend to be – with a brass band, majorettes and an annual 'sing' which started in 1885 and usually takes place in late June. It also has its Penistone Players, a still-active cinema, and not the least of its attractions, good parking.

The approach up the valley from Oxspring is enhanced by interesting stone viaducts, somewhat marred by ugly black

▲ Traditional crafts are demonstrated at Rowsley's Caudwell Mill

electricity pylons. The countryside to the north and west is magnificent.

ROWSLEY
MAP REF: 93SK2566

'The scenery is varied and beautiful – a combination of wood and water, and hill, dale and meadow.' No change has affected that 1895 description of Great Rowsley, where the A6 enters the National Park from the south across a 15th-century Derwent bridge. The bridge was widened in 1925 and stands just upstream of the river's confluence with the Wye. Great Rowsley is a village of gracious houses – almost all owned by the Duke of Rutland.

The Peacock, built as a private house in 1652, became an inn around 1828 and was described 20 years later as 'the beau ideal of an English country hostelry'. Then as now it was much favoured by anglers. The nearby Grouse and Claret, originally the Station Hotel, now correctly carries the sign of a fishing-fly – not the bird and drink that an earlier signwriter painted.

Caudwell's Mill on the Wye was operated by water-power from 1874 to 1978, and having been restored by volunteers is again using the roller-milling machinery that was installed early this century, to produce traditional wholemeal flour. The mill now also houses a busy craft centre, shops and a restaurant.

Little Rowsley, a railway colony of mainly red-brick houses, stands on the Chatsworth road east of the River Derwent and outside the National Park. Although the railway and its depot closed in the 1960s, Paxton's delightful station of 1849 survives on a small industrial estate.

RUDYARD
MAP REF: 80SJ9558

Less than half a mile west of the A523 and 3 miles north of Leek is Rudyard, a Victorian lakeside resort encircled by hills. Rudyard 'lake' is actually a reservoir that was constructed in 1799 to feed the Caldon Canal. From 1845 the North Staffordshire Railway Company, which had acquired the canal, developed the reservoir and old village as a pleasure resort. Excursion trains from Leek arrived at Rudyard every 15 minutes during bank holiday peak periods. On one day in 1877, 20,000 people went there to see Captain Webb swim.

Among those with particular reason to remember Rudyard were John Lockwood Kipling and his wife Alice, for it was there that they became engaged. In gratitude they named their son Rudyard, who later became the famous author.

Sailing and coarse fishing are available on the lake, and the 4-mile walk round it includes on the west shore a section of the Staffordshire Way footpath which

extends for 90 miles between Mow Cop and Kinver Edge. The road west from the lake goes to Horton, which has some interesting old houses and a mainly 16th-century church containing Wedgwood family monuments. The main road north passes through Rushton Spencer, where a fine railway station has been converted into a private house, and a hilltop church of many styles is sometimes known as 'the Chapel in the Wilderness'.

SHELDON
MAP REF: 92SK1768

A former lead-mining village, Sheldon clings to a steep hillside just below the rim of the limestone uplands at 1,000ft, its single street bordered by wide strips of green. The farmhouses and cottages behind the green date mainly from the 18th century, a time when its mining industry was flourishing.

The plateau above the village is dotted with prehistoric monuments and the remnants of lead mining, but the dominant feature is Magpie Mine – last worked (unsuccessfully) in 1958. Its buildings date from a century earlier, and it has records going back to 1739. Said to be both cursed and haunted, the mine was stabilised in the 1970s and is probably the best-preserved lead mine surviving in Britain. Visiting parties can be arranged through the Peak District Mining Museum at Matlock Bath, and it serves as a field centre for the Peak District Mines Historical Society.

West across the open fields is Flagg, a remote hamlet with a handsome Elizabethan Hall. The High Peak Hunt point-to-point races are held annually on Easter Tuesday at the edge of the parish, near the A515 road and close to the picturesque Bull I' Th' Thorn Inn – an interesting building which is believed to date from 1472.

▼ Magpie Mine is open to visitors

STANTON IN PEAK
MAP REF: 93SK2464

Long, steep, single-street hillside villages are numerous in Peakland, and Stanton in Peak, on the northern scarp of Stanton Moor, is typical – although the street curves more than others, and has numerous tributary alleyways and secluded courtyards.

The initials WPT over cottage doorways stand for William Paul Thornhill of Stanton Hall, which is still occupied by his Davie-Thornhill descendants behind a high wall near the church. His family gave the church to the village in 1839, along with a bronze holy-water stoup dated 1596. 'The Flying Childers' Inn is named after a successful racehorse owned by the 4th Duke of Devonshire.

Above the village is Stanton Moor, an isolated island of gritstone rising to 1,096ft from a limestone sea. On this long plateau are more than 70 barrows and cairns that were all excavated this century by a father and son team, the late J C and J P Heathcote of Birchover. Perhaps the most interesting feature is the stone circle known as the Nine Ladies. The solitary King's Stone standing nearby may be connected with it, but other upright stones on the moor are natural survivors from eroded millstone grit. The tower on Stanton Moor Edge was erected in 1832 in honour of Earl Grey's involvement in the passing of the Reform Act.

In a quite beautiful setting, the Nine Ladies stone circle on Stanton Moor is 33yds round ▼

▲ Sunset on Stanton Moor

STOCKSBRIDGE
MAP REF: 85SK2798

'How green was my valley once', one is tempted to quote as Deepcar merges into Stocksbridge without any noticeable change in the 2-mile dark ribbon of houses on either side of the A616 (T). The odd thing is that the valley of the River Porter – or Little Don – is still green on its higher northern slopes above the great steel works that frowns across at Stocksbridge. Even on the southern side above the road the steep hillside has been landscaped and converted into a pleasing stretch of public park, with seats where one can ruminate on this strange juxtaposition of ugliness and beauty.

The ugliness is only skin-deep. One mile north or south of the V-shaped valley lies open moorland; 2 miles south is the National Park boundary, and the wilderness of Broomhead and Bradfield Moor. Even west, the Stocksbridge sprawl halts abruptly at the dam wall of Underbank reservoir, beyond which is a long, open, scenic stretch of road through Langsett to Holmfirth.

Stocksbridge is the last fling of Sheffield and the steel country.

Two miles north-east in idyllic surroundings by the Don can be seen where and how it all began – at Wortley Top Forge (open on Sundays). This forge is typical of the little ironworks that laid the foundations of Sheffield's wealth back in monastic times.

Relying at first on just a few workers – perhaps only on one family – and on the power of hill streams, forges sprang up all around Sheffield. Wortley Top, which may have been working in medieval times, was definitely operative in 1695 and continued in production until 1929. Visitors to the forge today see the results of rebuilding in 1713, for both machinery and structure have been virtually unchanged since then.

STONEY MIDDLETON
MAP REF: 89SK2375

Stony it certainly is, with great natural walls of white limestone rising sheer from the floor of Middleton Dale and blocking the sunlight from the A623 road. Higher up the dale are two large quarries, and all around are disused ones – as well as traces of disused lead mines. The numerous

limekilns have gone, however, and with them the 'sulphur smells and thick smoke' that hung over both valley and village in the 18th century.

Stoney Middleton is now a clean, pleasant village of character, especially away from the main road around The Nook – a charming square where two wells are dressed in late July. Close by is a rare octagonal church with a lantern storey that was grafted on to a Perpendicular tower in 1759. The Jacobean Hall behind was the home of the Denmans – mostly distinguished surgeons, apart from one notable exception who became

Lord Chief Justice in 1832. He may have built the bath house whose ruins stand over thermal springs which the Romans may have used.

The present main road, still called New Road, was laid out by the turnpike trustees in 1840. The octagonal tollhouse of that date – a listed building – is now a fish and chip shop. Higher up is Lover's Leap, so called since 1762 when a jilted girl called Hannah Badderley tried to end it all by jumping from a high rock. Her voluminous skirt opened like a parachute and caught on brambles protruding from a ledge, where she hung suspended for a while before

rolling gently and only slightly injured into a saw-pit.

Stoney Middleton was once a boot- and shoe-making centre, and a surviving firm operates from a former corn mill. The largest source of employment is, however, the fluorspar industry – based 1,000ft up on the moors above the village. Nearly three-quarters of Britain's fluorspar – used in the production of steel, chemicals, ceramics and aluminium – is produced from a strip of limestone upland that extends south from the Hope valley almost to Matlock and Wirksworth, but is little more than a single mile wide.

CLIMBING COUNTRY

Frowning down on the broad shale valley of the Derwent for about 15 miles from Outer Edge in the north to Harland Edge in the south are the famous Peakland Eastern Edges.

These precipitous, castellated walls of gritstone, up to 60ft high in places like Stanage Edge near Hathersage, attract rock climbers from all over Britain. The firm, abrasive qualities of Peakland grit are highly regarded in the climbing world, and the severity of the routes which have been led on it is in a class out of all proportion to the modest elevations.

The edges are the eroded remains of a millstone grit cap, formed by the deltas of Carboniferous Age rivers, which once covered the limestone of the White Peak.

Many of the finest climbers Britain has produced first made their names on these rock walls, so close to the great northern cities from where they came. Men like Joe Brown and the late Don Whillans from Manchester took the sport of rock climbing to new extremes in the 1950s and 1960s, and many of their pioneering routes are still held in awe by climbers today.

Stanage is still the Mecca for the gritstone rock athlete, and on a sunny weekend, the 4 miles of crags can be festooned with brightly coloured ropes like streamers at a party. The names given to routes like the Right and Left Unconquerables have long since been proved inaccurate, and today over 500 other climbs exist along the weathered ramparts.

Over on the opposite side of the National Park, the edges of the western fringe are more shattered but offer climbing

routes every bit as severe in places. Among them are the Roaches, Hen Cloud and Windgather Rocks. Don Whillan's challenging overhang route, the Sloth (so-called because of the length of time spent hanging upside down) remains designated a classic 'hard very severe'.

Rock climbing began in the Peak District around the turn of the century with pioneers like J W Puttrell investigating the edges for their climbing potential for the first time. It could be said the sport was born here, although Lake District afficionados would probably dispute it. No one could deny though that this is where it blossomed, and several of its best climbers went on to become conquerors of Alpine and Himalayan giants, including Everest.

In later years, attention has increasingly been switched to the even longer and more exposed routes on the smooth limestone crags of the dales, which take the sport of rock climbing into ever greater extremes of athleticism and demand greater use of artificial aids in the conquest of new challenges.

For those who want nothing more than a pleasant stroll with outstanding views, the paths along the tops of the edges provide a breathtaking promenade – with the added interest of the remains of the forgotten industry of millstone making at their foot, and the antics of the climbers for company.

◀ Hanging on for dear life: Curbar's gritstone edge is popular with climbers

TADDINGTON
MAP REF: 92SK1471

As the A6 climbs sinously through Taddington Dale from Ashford its steep gradient is disguised by numerous bends and the thick woodlands on either side. Above the tree-line on the bare plateau it avoids the long, rising main street of Taddington by following one of the earliest Peakland village bypasses.

Taddington stands high, its cottages small and simple and its rather grand church commandingly sited at the top of the village. On the strength of prospering wool and lead trades, some splendid churches were built or rebuilt in the 14th century, with nearby Tideswell the supreme example. Taddington is smaller and less ambitious.

From the church, a footpath running west over Taddington Moor to Chelmorton reaches 1,438ft before passing close to Five Wells tumulus after 1½ miles – the highest megalithic tomb in England. On private land, the mound has eroded away to expose two burial chambers of limestone slabs. Inside were 12 inhumations, flint tools and scraps of pottery. The name is significant, for the numerous springs rising hereabouts account for the wealth of tumuli at this height – and also probably for the siting of Taddington.

North of the bypass is evidence of Celtic or early-Saxon terrace cultivation at Priestcliffe, in the form of stepped 'lynchets'.

TAXAL AND WHALEY BRIDGE
MAP REF: 86SK0079

Whaley Bridge is a small town, while Taxal consists merely of a church, the Chimes of Taxal Inn

◀ Taddington is one of the highest villages in England

(formerly the Royal Oak) and perhaps a dozen gritstone houses among trees on the west bank of the Goyt. Taxal, however, is the senior partner by many centuries. Its church remains the parish church and its large churchyard the official cemetery for Whaley Bridge – which was a cotton-weaving town and is now concerned with engineering and clothing.

Although a boundary change in 1936 transferred Taxal from Cheshire to Derbyshire, it remains in the Diocese of Chester and the Province of York – except for the hamlet of Fernilee across the Goyt, which is in Derby Diocese in Canterbury Province but regards Taxal as its parish church. The large parish extends virtually from Lyme Park in the north to the Cat and Fiddle in the south, and from Rainow on the west to Chapel-en-le-Frith in the east.

Windgather Rocks, overlooking Taxal in the west, are a favourite training-ground for rock climbers. Beyond them is the little village of Kettleshulme, where candlewicks were made until 1937. The Bow Stones, a mile north-west of Kettleshulme, may have been used for stringing bows – though a rival theory is that they mark the boundary of Macclesfield Forest.

South of Kettleshulme at Saltersford is the isolated Jenkin Chapel of 1733, which has domestic windows and chimney, and a saddleback tower that was added in 1755. It also retains its original box pews, pulpit and reading desk. An open-air harvest-festival service is usually held here sometime in September.

The Cromford and High Peak Railway used to drop dramatically down an inclined plane to its northern terminus at the Whaley Bridge basin on the Peak Forest Canal. The basin has now been restored and is used as a marina.

TIDESWELL
MAP REF: 88SK1575

Tideswell Church is often described as 'the Cathedral of the Peak'. The splendid cruciform building was erected between about 1300 and 1370, with just a short break immediately after the Black Death, so it is almost wholly in the Decorated style. Only the soaring and pinnacled west tower – which is in the Perpendicular style – and just a few hints of changing

architectural trends in the chancel are the exceptions.

The whole church is spacious and lofty, the tower arch and the east and west windows being exceptionally tall. Its chancel is rich in pre-Reformation tombs and brasses, and the building displays a wealth of wood carving – mainly 19th-century work by Suffolk carvers and local man Advent Hunstone, whose nephew continues the family tradition in the present century.

Tideswell is in fact a village of craftsmen, working on their own in buildings converted from other uses. This is apparent from the excellence of its well-dressing, which starts – along with the week-long wakes – on the Saturday which falls nearest St John the Baptist's Day.

▲ Tideswell's shops boast goods made by local craftsmen

Architecturally the village tends to suffer by comparison with its glorious church, and it is often underrated. Exploration of its streets and alleyways is most rewarding, however, with many of the buildings revealing that they are far older than they look.

The late 18th-century George Hotel – with its Venetian windows – and both Blake House and Eccles Hall are especially interesting. The gardens of 'Welyards' in Sherwood Road are frequently open and worth seeing, but it is a waste of time looking for the ebbing and flowing well, which ceased to do either of these things when piped water arrived many years ago.

Tideswell received a market charter in 1250. It flourished in the wool and lead trades during the 14th century – which explains the lavishness of the church – but then declined to village status and, luckily, became too poor to update its church. North-west of Tideswell, in the hamlet of Wheston, are a small but complete 15th-century village cross, a dilapidated and 'haunted' 16th- and 17th-century hall, and several interesting old farmhouses.

TINTWISTLE AND LONGDENDALE

MAP REF: 82SK0297

Tintwistle is another 'last outpost of civilisation' – the final link in a chain of 19th-century cotton towns and villages that began miles to the north-west in central Lancashire, and petered out on the western boundary of the National Park where the wilderness of Longdendale begins. It was a small, gritstone village when the domestic cotton industry arrived in around 1750. It trebled its population between 1801 and 1851, when the first mills were built.

The mills have gone and the population has halved, but terraces of weavers' cottages survive in Higher Square, Lower Square and Chapel Brow at the older, unplanned eastern end of the village. There, from a sloping green 800ft above sea level, can be enjoyed an impressive view across Bottoms reservoir to the encircling hills of Longdendale.

Bottoms is the lowest in a chain of five reservoirs, which with two more west of Tintwistle, were constructed for Manchester Corporation along the valley of Longdendale over a 30-year period from 1848. The work followed almost immediately after completion of the first two Woodhead tunnels on the Manchester-to-Sheffield section of what became the Great Central Line. During the operation some 32 labourers died (mainly of cholera), and there were countless injuries. When a third tunnel opened in 1954 to take the newly electrified line, the first two were closed. One of these was re-opened in the 1960s to take electric transmission lines and so avoid further scarring of the Longdendale landscape.

Since then the railway service has ended. The threat of a motorway through Longdendale has so far been averted, but the threat of a pumped storage plant at Robinson's Moss still hangs over this blemished but still beautiful valley. Walking in the surrounding hills is wonderful for experienced people with the right equipment.

The Pennine Way drops down to Crowden Youth Hostel – overlooking Torside reservoir, where there is sailing – and then climbs north again to Black Hill (1,908ft).

The Norman tower of St Mary's Church at Tissington is visible from the green. The nave was restored in 1854 ▶

TISSINGTON AND FENNY BENTLEY

MAP REF: 95SK1752

Many people consider Tissington to be the most beautiful village in the National Park, and well-dressing enthusiasts revere it as the birthplace of the traditional craft.

It has everything the tourist desires – a Norman church on a mound facing a splendid Jacobean manor house, ducks sailing serenely on the village mere, cheerful limestone houses set back behind wide strips of green and five attractive wells which – together with a children's well – are all dressed on Ascension Day.

The whole village has been carefully managed by the Fitzherbert family since the reign of Elizabeth I. From the original manor house on the site of an Iron Age fort next to the church, they moved across the road to their newly built home at Tissington Hall in about 1610. They extended the hall in Georgian times, then again early this century, and rebuilt most of the other houses in the traditional local style between about 1830 and 1860. The church was perhaps over-restored in 1854.

Fenny Bentley straddles the winding A515 about 2 miles away and is the Peak's southernmost village. Its smattering of Midland-clay brick houses is scattered among more numerous stone ones, and although the village has not had a resident squire for three centuries its interesting medieval church is still dominated by the Beresfords – one-time chief family. Thomas, who survived Agincourt and lived another 58 years, shares an impressive alabaster tomb-chest with his wife and their 21 children (all covered in shrouds round the sides).

Their descendants attend an annual reunion of the Beresford Family Society, and parts of their medieval moated manor house are incorporated into Cherry Orchard Farm. A massive square tower, like a defensive Northumbrian pele tower, may have been part of a gatehouse.

Tissington Trail crosses Bentley Hill between the villages on its way to Tissington's former railway station, where there is a car park, a picnic site and refreshments. Nearby are excellent examples of the old open-field farming system.

▼ Fenny Bentley's church sundial

FARMING IN THE PEAK

Man has been farming in the Peak District for well over 5,000 years, and the landscape admired by visitors today is largely the creation of successive generations of farmers.

Forest clearance began in Mesolithic times, on the now bleak, open moorlands of the Dark Peak and rolling upland pastures of the White Peak limestone plateau. In fact, it is probably only in the rocky gritstone cloughs and crags of the limestone dales which are inaccessible to grazing animals that a truly natural landscape, untouched by man, can be found today.

Farming is still the most important single industry in the Peak District, although the number of people employed by it is decreasing through mechanisation and the demise of many small family farms. In an upland area like the Peak District, the most typical form of farming is pastoral, and livestock enterprises predominate. Dairying and sheep are most common on the limestone plateau, although on the lower slopes – especially around Bakewell – an increasing amount of land has been turned over to arable crops, particularly the alien mustard-yellow oilseed rape.

Concrete-lined dewponds, locally known as meres, have been constructed over the years to catch the precious rainwater and to provide water for stock. Perhaps the most distinctive feature are the miles and miles of drystone walls which spread over the gently swelling contours like a net, keeping the stock from straying. Most were constructed by the Enclosure Acts of the late 18th and early 19th centuries, when open moorland was parcelled off.

Recent research has shown, however, that some walls are much older than this, and may go back to medieval or even Roman times. Certainly, sheep and cattle have been kept on these limestone pastures for many centuries, and although the traditional economies of mining and farming are seldom practised today, they remain two of the most important sources of employment.

On the Dark Peak moorlands, sheep reign supreme and share their lofty heather-clad pastures with the red grouse, which are shot annually after the 'Glorious 12th' of August. The Peak District is the home of two specialist breeds of mountain sheep bred to withstand the rigours of the harsh Dark Peak winters. They are the polled, speckle-faced Derbyshire Gritstone, originally known as the Dale O'Goyt, and the large Roman-nosed Whitefaced Woodland, from the Woodlands valley in the north of the district.

Drystone walling has been called a dying art, but there are many seasoned practitioners around who can still build a mortarless wall which will stand for two centuries. So important a feature are these lasting monuments that the National Park authority pays farmers under management agreements to ensure their upkeep and maintenance.

A pastoral scene at Wetton. Hares often appear hereabouts, bounding up the scree-scattered slopes ▼

◄ Mermaid Pool is said to be bottomless

MAP REF: 94SK0858

For dramatic effect, these two places are best seen in reverse order. A minor road running south from the Mermaid Inn seems to drop through a hole in the moors, and the houses of Upper Elkstone cling grimly to the steep, spiral route. Unexpectedly simple, the towerless and aisleless village church is on a level platform. Behind its round-headed sash windows are box pews, a gallery, a

▲ Wild boars once roamed the glades around Wildboarclough. According to local tradition, this was where the last wild boar was killed, rendering them extinct in Britain

two-decker pulpit and the Royal Arms of George III – all dating from 1786. It also has a Morris window of 1922.

At the foot of the hill are a few farmhouses that make up Lower Elkstone in the remote green valley of Warslow Brook. It is a different world from both the bare moorlands above and the populous Potteries 15 miles away.

By comparison Warslow seems large and sophisticated. It is in fact a pleasantly leafy, stone-built estate village with a church of 1820 provided by Sir George Crewe – of Calke Abbey. Its chancel was added in 1908, and it features much 20th-century stained glass by William Morris & Co. Sir George built Warslow Hall, 1½ miles outside the village on the Longnor road, as a shooting box.

▼ The Mermaid Inn near Warslow

WATERHOUSES
MAP REF: 94SK0850

A footpath along the Hamps and Manifold valleys starts from a car park on the north side of the A523 Ashbourne-to-Leek road. The road keeps company with the Hamps

part of the way through this straggling village, which was once a terminus of the now-defunct Manifold Valley Light Railway.

South at Cauldon is a large and too-prominent cement works close to Cauldon Low, a hill which has been almost munched away by quarrying. Some of the disused quarries provide interesting rockface profiles, visible from an award-winning craft centre and health-food restaurant housed in a former school in Cauldon Lowe village. Away from this small industrial belt the surrounding countryside is splendid and worthy of exploration.

WILDBOARCLOUGH
MAP REF: 90SJ9868

The last wild boar was reputedly hunted to extinction here in the 15th century, and the last of three mid 18th-century mills that turned the village into an outpost of the Macclesfield silk industry – and later made carpets exhibited at the Great Exhibition of 1851 – was demolished in 1958. The only road through the clough is below Shutlingsloe (1,659ft). It is still attended by its chain of little waterfalls on Clough Brook, which swelled to create a disastrous flood in 1989. Fortunately, Wildboarclough is still an attractive little village in gorgeously remote countryside.

James Brindley, later of canal fame, installed the machinery at

the village's first silk mill while apprenticed to Abraham Bennett of Sutton, near Macclesfield. Although the mill has gone, the administrative building has survived.

Clough Brook turned the wheels of a vanished paper mill at Allgreave, just before its confluence with the Dane – which powered another paper mill at Wincle, between Back Dane and the attractive hamlet of Danebridge. At Gradbach, one mile up the Dane before its junction with the brook, a former 18th-century silk mill (rebuilt after a fire in 1785 and converted into a saw mill by Sir John Harpur Crewe in the 1870s), has been converted into a Youth Hostel.

A track running west from Gradbach ends close to Lud's Church, which is an extraordinary cleft between walls of rock 20ft apart on the edge of Back Forest. It was a secret place of worship for Wycliffe's Lollards in the 14th century, taking its name – apparently – from Walter de Lud-Auk and setting part of the scene, according to recent research, for the famous medieval poem *Sir Gawain and the Green Knight*. Lud's Church has been identified as the Green Chapel, and the medieval hunting lodge of Swythamley Hall as the site of the Green Knight's castle. Swythamley Hall was rebuilt by the Brocklehurst family during the mid 19th century.

▲ Winster's Church of St John the Baptist is unusual in that it has two aisles

WINSTER
MAP REF: 93SK2460

Winster may have lost its town status and weekly market, but it retains its dignity and urbanity. It has also kept its charming market hall, the most conspicuous of its buildings because it protrudes into Main Street. The 16th-century ground floor was once open, as at Chipping Campden, Ross-on-Wye and Bakewell, but the space between the pointed arches has been filled in. The brick upper storey, added a century later, houses an information centre and a shop belonging to the National Trust – who bought it in 1906 as its first purchase in Derbyshire or the Peak. It is open at weekends and on bank holidays from April to September.

Other imposing houses, nearly all with three storeys, can be seen in Main Street. Those on East Bank and West Bank date mostly from the 18th-century heyday of local lead mining. The double-gabled Dower House, at the west end of Main Street, is a century earlier. Less dignified but no less endearing are the little alleyways or 'ginnels', running off Main Street and up the sheltering cliffside.

A bell summons Winster housewives to an annual Shrove Tuesday pancake race. There is also a village market on summer bank holidays and a week of wakes festivities takes place at the end of June – as well as morris dancing at various times of the year.

Just out of the village on the B5056, near the top of West Bank, is the Miner's Standard Inn – which takes its name from the standard dish used by miners for measuring lead ore (see Wirksworth). Appropriately, the

Visitors can watch reproduction antique furniture being made in Wirksworth ▶

area is riddled with old lead-mine shafts and hillocks. A mile east of Winster is the pretty limestone village of Wensley, on a hillside where the B5057 drops from Wensley Dale to cross the River Derwent at Darley Bridge.

WIRKSWORTH
MAP REF: 81SK2854

In about 1720 Daniel Defoe saw Wirksworth as 'a kind of market for lead: the like not known anywhere else that I know of. . . .' – but the lead industry died, and Wirksworth almost expired with it. Now, thanks to a Civic Trust Project and a lot of hard work by the Derbyshire Historic Buildings Trust and many other bodies, it has been reborn and seems destined to become an important tourist centre.

It has the natural advantage of a good position in a bowl of the hills at the head of the Ecclesbourne valley, where a number of minor roads meet. Two of them curve uphill to meet by a crazily tilted market place. It also has a minor part in literary history as the Snowfield of *Adam Bede*, and the home of author George Eliot's aunt, Elizabeth Evans – the model for Dinah Bede. Hers was the first house on the right as the town is entered by the Derby road.

The splendid church in a most charming circular mini-close is already a tourist attraction, mainly because of what is probably the Peak's earliest Christian monument – a coffin lid discovered in 1820 but dating from the late 7th century.

Moot Hall, which was rebuilt in 1812, is where the Barmote Court still meets twice annually to settle lead-mining disputes – as it is known to have done since 1266 and almost certainly has for much longer. A standard measuring dish

holding 14 pints of ore and made in 1512 hangs on the wall. The Heritage Centre in a former silk and velvet mill off the Market Place deals with most aspects of local life.

Wirksworth dresses nine wells on late spring bank holiday Saturday, which coincides with the annual carnival. The annual ceremony of clypping (embracing) the church takes place on the Sunday after 8 September.

Middleton-by-Wirksworth, 1½ miles north-west, is a hillside quarrying village of character which has a huge and rare limestone mine. The famous Hopton Wood Marble (a form of limestone) from Middleton has been used in such buildings as Westminster Abbey, York Minster

and the Houses of Parliament, and for headstones in war cemeteries. Above the village is Middleton Top Engine House, on the High Peak Trail. It has a beam engine built at the Ripley Butterley Works in 1829.

Along the road between Middleton and Black Rocks is the new National Stone Centre, opened in 1990, which tells the story of stone from earliest times. Open all year, it has ambitious plans for future development.

WORMHILL
MAP REF: 91SK1274

Midway between Buxton and Tideswell and directly above Chee Dale, Wormhill is not so much a village as an extended collection of handsome old farmhouses climbing a minor road to more than 1,000ft at Wormhill Hill. On the road north to Hargatewall is Old Hall Farm, which dates from the 16th and 17th centuries and was probably a manor house before the present H-shaped hall was built at the foot of the hill in 1697. Behind the hall at a higher level is the church, which was rebuilt in 1864 and capped by a Rhineland-style tower – perhaps inspired by the Saxon helm-tower a long way south at Sompting in Sussex.

On the green in 1895 an ornate stone structure was erected round a well in rather belated memory of 'James Brindley, Civil Engineer, Born in this Parish AD 1716'. His cottage birthplace at Tunstead was demolished shortly after his death in 1772 because a persistent ash tree kept growing through the floor. His well is dressed annually

▲ Wormhill Hall was restored by the Bagshawes, who have lived in the area for centuries

on the Saturday falling before the late August bank holiday.

The views from Wormhill are spectacular, though to the west they are dominated by the quarries of Great Rocks Dale, which threaten to encroach into the parish.

YOULGREAVE
MAP REF: 92SK2164

There may be doubts about the spelling – more than 60 versions exist – but none at all about the charm of this extended village, which runs along a shelf of fairly

► Top: Youlgreave and its Church of All Saints. The alabaster tomb inside (inset) is of Thomas Cokayne, who died in 1488. ►

level ground between the Bradford and Lathkill Rivers before they join. Behind the cottages on the south side of the long, narrow street (which has been called 'England's longest car park'), are pretty, private gardens that tumble down to the Bradford. It flows so close below the cliff as to be invisible from above. A road by the church and numerous alleyways and stone steps lead down to the river, which is spanned in quick succession by a packhorse bridge, a clapper bridge and a rather more modern road bridge.

The church juts out into the main street, and from some angles its splendid Perpendicular tower appears to block the roadway. Its wide nave is mainly Norman, as is the large tub-font with a rare attached stoop for oil. Among an interesting collection of monuments is a mini-tomb and mini-effigy in alabaster to Thomas Cockayne, killed in a teenage brawl in 1488.

Near the church are some rather grand Georgian houses, while farther west is the Old Hall – a long, low, mullioned building that is typical of the White Peak and dated 1656. It may be older. Behind it, screened from the street, is the Old Hall Farm of around 1630. A marvellous, three-storey shop built for the local Co-operative Society in 1887 now serves as a youth hostel.

Facing it from the site of a Saxon cross is an oval gritstone water tank officially called the Conduit Head, and unofficially the Fountain. This was built in 1829 by the village's own water company to supply soft water to all who paid sixpence annually. The boon was celebrated by Youlgreave's first known well-dressing in 1829. It now dresses five wells to a remarkably high standard even compared with the superb showpieces for which other Peak villages are famous, and still operates its own water-supply company.

East of the village the road drops to Alport, once a mill settlement making industrial use of the two rivers, but now a pretty little residential village much visited by artists. West along the river, where Bradford Dale becomes Middleton Dale, is Middleton-by-Youlgreave. Equally pretty, it is also exceptionally well-blessed with trees for the normally fairly unforested White Peak.

Lomberdale Hall, just outside the village, was the home of Thomas Bateman – the Victorian archaeologist of the area. His grave – appropriately surmounted by a Bronze Age urn – stands alone in a field. He excavated over 500 barrows in 20 years, and the artefacts he discovered are exhibited mainly in Sheffield's interesting Weston Park Museum.

◀ Calke Abbey, built between 1701 and 1703 for Sir John Harpur

PLACES TO VISIT

This is just a selection of the many places to visit in the Peak District. Each attraction is listed under its nearest town or village.

The details given are intended to provide a rough guide only to opening times. Some attractions may only be open for part of the day. Many places which are otherwise open all year are closed over Christmas and the New Year.

Full information should be obtained in advance of a visit from a local tourist information centre (see pages 74–5).

Many places are owned by The National Trust or are in the care of English Heritage, and if this is the case the entry is accompanied by the abbreviation NT or EH.

Telephone numbers are given in brackets.

BH = bank holiday
Etr = Easter

FACT FILE
CONTENTS

Places to Visit
Stately homes, castles, gardens, museums, theme parks and other attractions

Sports and Activities
Angling, cycling, golf, riding and trekking, watersports, walking

Useful Information
Addresses, tourist information centres, market days, theatres and cinemas

Craft Shops
A selection of workshops where original craft items are made

Customs and Events
A calendar

ALTON

Alton Towers. *Huge leisure park and gardens.* Open Etr to early Nov, daily. Gardens open all year.

BAKEWELL

The Old House Museum, off Church La. *Fine Tudor building housing rural bygones.* Open Apr to Oct, daily.

BRADWELL

Bagshawe Cavern. *System of show caves.* Open Jun and Jul, Sun; all year by appointment.

BUXTON

Micrarium, The Crescent. *Nature viewed through remote-controlled telescopes.* Open end Mar to early Nov, daily.

Museum and Art Gallery. *History of the Peak District.* Open all year, Tue to Sun.

Poole's Cavern, Buxton Country Park. *Cavern with video show and Roman exhibition.* Open Etr to Oct, daily. Closed Wed in Apr, May and Oct.

CALKE

Calke Abbey and Park (NT). *Baroque mansion with extensive wooded parkland.* Open Apr to Oct, Sat to Wed and BH Mon.

CASTLETON

Blue John Cavern and Mine. *Chambers 200ft high, with Blue John stone.* Open all year, daily.

▲ Chatsworth House, the 'Palace of the Peak', is the imposing seat of the Dukes of Devonshire. Begun in 1686, it is a vast classical mansion in grounds landscaped by Capability Brown

Cavendish House Museum. *Collection of Derbyshire treasures, including Blue John.* Open all year, daily.

Chestnut Centre, off A625 between Castleton and Chapel-en-le-Frith. *Sanctuary for otters, owls and falcons.* Open Etr to Oct, daily; winter weekends only.

Peak Cavern. *Spectacular limestone cave with underground walk.* Open Etr to Oct, daily.

Peveril Castle (EH). *Ruined castle above the town.* Open all year, Apr to Sep, daily; Oct to Etr, Tue to Sun.

Speedwell Cavern. *Underground exploration by boat.* Open all year, daily.

Treak Cliff Cavern and Mine. *Natural and artificial excavations.* Open all year, daily.

CHATSWORTH

Chatsworth House. *Palatial mansion with extensive grounds and other attractions.* Open end Mar to early Oct, daily.

CHEDDLETON

SEE LEEK

CHESTERFIELD

Peacock Information and Heritage Centre, Low Pavement. *Medieval building with displays on the town's history.* Open all year, Mon to Sat.

▲ Sir Richard Arkwright (1732–92), the cotton manufacturer

CROMFORD

Cromford Mill, Mill La. *Arkwright's cotton mill.* Open all year, daily.

High Peak Junction Workshops, Lea Rd. *Restored workshops of the Cromford and High Peak Railway.* Open all year, weekends.

DISLEY

Lyme Hall and Park (NT). *Huge estate with red and fallow deer.* House open Etr to Sep at varying times, sometimes guided tours only. Grounds open all year, daily.

LEEK

Flint Mill, Cheddleton. *Two old mills and a museum.* Open all year, daily.

North Staffordshire Steam Railway Centre, Cheddleton. *Railway museum in Jacobean-style station.* Open Etr to Sep, daily.

MACCLESFIELD

Heritage Centre. *Town history exhibition in former Sunday School.* Open all year, daily.

Museum and Art Gallery, West Park, Prestbury Rd. *Egyptian artefacts and works by Tunnicliffe and Landseer.* Open Etr to Sep, daily.

MATLOCK

Aquarium and Hologram. *Includes thermal pool where fish may be fed.* Open Etr to Oct, daily; winter, weekends only.

Gulliver's Kingdom and Royal Cave, Matlock Bath. *Theme park with rides and attractions.* Open Etr to mid Sep, daily.

Heights of Abraham, Matlock Bath. *Cable cars run up to this superb vantage point with landscaped gardens and other amenities.* Open Etr to Oct, daily.

Model Railway Museum, Temple Rd, Matlock Bath. *Railway relics.* Open Apr to Sep, Tue to Sun; Mon to Thu, Sat and Sun.

Peak District Mining Museum, The Pavilion, Matlock Bath. *History of the area's lead industry.* Open all year, daily.

Riber Castle Wildlife Park, Matlock. *Rare breeds and endangered species of European birds and animals.* Open all year, daily.

Temple Mine, Temple Road, Matlock Bath. *Restored lead workings.* Open Etr to Oᶜt, daily; Oct to Nov, Jan to Etr, weekends only.

MIDDLETON BY WIRKSWORTH

Middleton Top Engine House. *Beam engine built for the Cromford & High Peak Railway.* Engine House open Etr to Oct, Sun only. Visitor centre Etr to Sep, daily; Oct to Mar, weekends only.

NEW MILLS

Heritage and Information Centre, Rock Mill La. *Simulated coal mine and model of the town as it was in 1884, plus displays and videos.* Open all year, Tue to Sun and BH Mon.

ROWSLEY

Haddon Hall. *Romantic, ancient manor house.* Open Apr to Sep, daily (except Mon and Sun in Jul and Aug).

WIRKSWORTH

Wirksworth Heritage Centre, Crown Yd. *Interpretive displays and craftsmen.* Open Feb to Jun and Oct to mid Dec, Tue to Sun; Jun to Sep, Mon to Sun.

SPORTS AND ACTIVITIES

ANGLING

Most of the rivers in the Peak District are free from pollution and provide a wide choice of fishing locations. The limestone rivers are prime trout streams, and the Derwent and the Dove provide some of the best fly fishing.

The fishing rights on all waters are controlled, and permission to fish must always be obtained beforehand.

Whenever fishing on inland water, a rod licence must be obtained from the local region of the National Rivers Authority. Most waters in the Peak District National Park fall

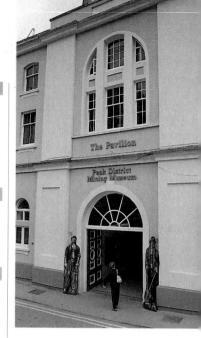

▲ The handsome façade of the Mining Museum at Matlock Bath

within the area of the Severn-Trent Region, although for the Yorkshire part of the Park licences are available from Rivers House, 21 Park Square South, Leeds LS1 2QG.

Fishing is also available on many of the reservoirs in the Park, and day tickets can be purchased at a number of these.

CYCLING

Disused railway tracks in the Peak District make ideal cycling routes. Cycle hire centres can be found at Ashbourne, Derwent, Parsley Hay and Waterhouses.

GOLF

The following clubs and courses welcome visitors:

A charming combination of medieval and Elizabethan architectural styles, Haddon Hall stands overlooking the Wye ▼

Ashbourne, *Ashbourne,* at Clifton, 1½ miles SW of Ashbourne (0335 42078).

Bakewell, *Bakewell,* off Station Rd (0629 812307).

Bamford, *Sickleholme,* ¾ mile S of Bamford (0443 51306).

Buxton, *Buxton & High Peak,* Town End, Fairfield, 1 mile NE of Buxton (0298 23453).

Cavendish, Gadley Lane, ¾ mile W of town centre (0298 23494).

Chapel-en-le-Frith, *Chapel-en-le-Frith,* The Cockyard, Manchester Road, ½ mile N of Chapel-en-le-Frith (0298 812118).

Chesterfield, *Chesterfield,* Walton, 2 miles SW of Chesterfield (0246 279256).

Stanedge, Walton Hay Farm, Walton, 5 miles SW of Chesterfield (0246 566156).
Tapton Park, Murray House, Tapton, ½ mile E of Chesterfield (0246 273887).

Glossop, *Glossop and District,* Hurst Lane, 1 mile E of Glossop (04574 3117).

Leek, *Leek,* Birchall, ¾ mile S of Leek (0538 384779).

Macclesfield, *Macclesfield,* The Hollins (0625 23227).

▲ Wirksworth Heritage Centre has a working smithy and other crafts on display. It is an entire community

Matlock, *Matlock,* Chesterfield Road, 1 mile NE of Matlock (0629 582191).

Mellor, *Mellor & Townscliffe,* Gibb Lane, Tarden, ½ mile S of Mellor (061-427 2208).

New Mills, *New Mills,* Shaw Marsh, ½ mile N of New Mills (0663 743485).

RIDING AND TREKKING

Buxton, Buxton Riding School, Fern Farm, Fern Road (0298 72319).

Northfield Farm, Flash, near Buxton (0298 22543).

Curbar, *Curbar Riding School,* Emberbrook, Bar Road (0433 30584).

Edale, *Ladybooth Trekking Centre,* Edale (0433 70205).
Mount Pleasant Farm, Biggin-by-Hartington (033525 436).

Leek, *Moorlands Trail Riding,* The Mill, Winkhill (0538 308638).

Matlock, *Hopkin Farm,* Tansley (0935 582253).
Red House Stables, Darley Dale (0935 733583).

▼ Grindleford Bridge spans the River Derwent at a junction of moorland roads

▲ The Cromford Canal

WATERSPORTS

Although there are no natural lakes within the Peak District, there are several reservoirs where sailing, windsurfing and waterskiing are available through organised clubs. Use by members of the public is not necessarily excluded, and further information can be obtained from the following addresses:

Bottoms Reservoir, *Bottoms Watersports Centre,* Woodhead Road, Tintwistle, Hadfield, Cheshire SK14 7HR (04574 64566).

Damflask Reservoir, *Sheffield Viking Sailing Club,* 92 Silverdale Road, Sheffield S11 9JL (0625 875336).

Dove Stone Reservoir, *Dove Stone Sailing Club,* Longrigging Farm, Booth, Halifax HX2 6SZ (0422 882908).

Ernwood Reservoir, *Ward Breck,* The Wash, Chapel-en-le-Frith, Stockport SK12 6QL (0663 50445).

Rudyard Lake, *Rudyard Lake Information Centre,* Lake Road, Rudyard, Leek, Staffs ST13 8XB (053833 280).

Torside Reservoir, *Glossop and District Sailing Club,* 24 Bowlacre Road, Gee Cross, Hyde, Cheshire SK14 5ES.

WALKING

The Peak District is criss-crossed with trails, which are often well laid-out and signposted. Several follow the tracks of former railways. Brief details of some of the established trails follow, and more information is obtainable from the National Park Head Office (see Addresses). Centres will also provide details of Ranger-led walks and organised discovery trails exploring particular subjects.

High Peak Trail. Runs from High Peak Junction near Cromford to Parsley Hay, and on to Dowlow, near Buxton.

Manifold Track. Follows the Manifold valley from the A523 near Waterhouses.

Monsal Trail. This trail follows the valley of the Wye on its route from Blackwell, via Monsal Head, to Bakewell.

Pennine Way. The longest long-distance footpath in the country, running from Edale to the Scottish border. Not to be tackled by inexperienced walkers.

Sett Valley. A short walk crossing the Park from east to west following the former Hayfield to New Mills railway.

Tissington Trail. This runs from Ashbourne to meet the High Peak Trail at Parsley Hay.

USEFUL INFORMATION
ADDRESSES

English Heritage, Finchfield House, Castlecroft Road, Wolverhampton WV3 8BY (0902 765105).

The National Trust, Regional Office, East Midlands, Clumber Park Stableyard, Worksop, Notts S80 3BE (0909 486411).

Peak District National Park, National Park Head Office, Aldern House, Baslow Road, Bakewell, Derbys DE4 1AE (0629 814321).

Tourist Board, East Midlands Tourist Board, Exchequergate, Lincoln LN2 1PZ (0522 32501).

TOURIST INFORMATION CENTRES

Ashbourne, 13 Market Place (0335 43666).

Bakewell, Old Market Hall, Bridge Street (0629 813227).

Buxton, The Crescent (0298 25106).

Castleton, Castle Street (0433 20679).

▼ Thorpe Cloud has spectacular views across Dovedale

▲ The start of the Pennine Way in Edale. The footpath covers 250 miles of England's wildest and most beautiful countryside

Chesterfield, Peacock Information and Heritage Centre, Low Pavement (0246 207777).

Derby, Assembly Rooms, Market Place (0332 255802).

Derwent Valley, Fairholmes (0433 50953).

Edale, Fieldhead (0433 70207).

Glossop, Station Forecourt, Norfolk Street (0457 855920).

Matlock Bath, The Pavilion (0629 55082).

MARKET DAYS

Bakewell, Monday
Bolsover, Tuesday and Friday
Buxton, Tuesday and Saturday
Chapel-en-le-Frith, Thursday
Chesterfield, Monday, Thursday, Friday and Saturday
Glossop, Thursday, Friday and Saturday
The Matlocks, Tuesday and Friday
New Mills, Thursday, Friday and Saturday
Wirksworth, Tuesday

THEATRES AND CINEMAS

There are theatres at Buxton, Chesterfield, Derby and Manchester, and cinemas at Chesterfield, Derby, Macclesfield and Matlock.

CRAFT SHOPS

This is just a selection of the craft shops to be found throughout the region.

Ashbourne, Derwent Crystal, Shaw Croft car park. *Visitors can watch glass being blown and decorated.*

Bakewell, Lathkill Dale Craft Centre, Over Haddon. *All sorts of craft items, including stained glass and baby clothes.*

Calver Bridge, Derbyshire Craft Centre, 2 miles N of Baslow. *Local and national craft items for sale.*

Hartington, Rooke's Pottery. *Original terracotta ware made and sold.*

Longnor, Longnor Craft Centre, The Market Hall. *Solid oak and elm range of furniture, plus other crafts.*

▼ Bakewell's Monday market is bustling and full of colour.

▲ **Rowsley, Caudwell's Mill Craft Centre.** *Wood-turning, ceramics, glass-blowers, clock-maker etc.*

Tideswell, The Tideswell Dale Rock Shop, Commercial Road. *Ashford 'black marble' worked in the traditional manner. Also ornaments made of Blue John.*

Waterhouses, Staffordshire Peaks Arts Centre. *Wide variety of paintings and crafts. Exhibitions.*

Youlgreave, Asquith Silver. *Modern silverware and jewellery made and sold.*

CUSTOMS AND EVENTS

Although the events shown in this section usually take place in the months under which they appear, the actual dates of many vary from year to year.

Numerous other events, such as fêtes, county shows, flower festivals and horse shows also take place regularly in the area.

Full details of exactly what is happening, where can be obtained from tourist information centres (see pages 74–5) and local newspapers.

FEBRUARY

Shrovetide Football, Ashbourne (Shrove Tuesday and Ash Wednesday). *Free-for-all between two teams living either side of the town.*

MAY

Castleton Garland Day, Castleton (29th). *The garlanded 'king' proceeds through the streets to the church, where the garland is placed on the tower.*

Endon Well Dressing, Endon, near Leek (Spring BH). *Includes a thanksgiving service, maypole and morris dancing.*

Tissington Well Dressing, Tissington (Ascension Day). *Traditional dressing of well.*

JUNE

Derbyshire County Show, Derby (third week).

Hope Wakes and Well Dressing, Hope (last Saturday, for one week). *Parades, floats, well blessing.*

Tideswell Wakes Week and Well Dressing, Tideswell.

JULY

Bakewell Well Dressing and Carnival Week, Bakewell. *Races, competitions, events, processions.*

Buxton International Arts Festival, Buxton (mid July to early August). *Performances of the arts.*

Buxton Well Dressing, Buxton (second Wednesday, for four days). *Festival week with carnival and processions.*

AUGUST

Plague Sunday, Eyam (last Sunday). *Open-air service to commemorate the plague in Eyam in 1665.*

Well Dressing, Barlow (Wednesday after second Sunday). *Three separate dressings, and a blessing service.*

SEPTEMBER

Chatsworth Country Fair, Chatsworth. *Attractions for all the family.*

Clypping of the Parish, Wirksworth. *St Mary's Church is embraced with a circle of hands; service.*

Many hours of work are required to make a well dressing. This fine example was created in Hope in Derbyshire ▼

Atlas

▲ Goyt Valley

The following pages contain a legend, key map and atlas of the Peak District, three circular motor tours and sixteen planned walks.

MAP SYMBOLS

THE GRID SYSTEM

The map references used in this book are based on the Ordnance Survey National Grid, correct to within 1000 metres. They comprise two letters and four figures, and are preceded by the atlas page number.

Thus the reference for Buxton appears **91 SK 0673**

91 is the atlas page number

SK identifies the major (100km) grid square concerned (see diag)

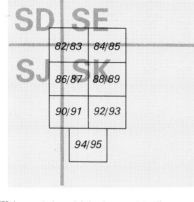

```
SD | SE
     82/83 | 84/85
SJ | SK
     86/87 | 88/89
     90/91 | 92/93
            94/95
```

0673 locates the lower left-hand corner of the kilometre grid square in which Buxton appears

06 can be found along the bottom edge of the page, reading W to E

73 can be found along the right hand side of the page, reading S to N

```
          |        |     74
          | o Buxton|
          |        |     73
          |        |     72
   05     06      07
```

ATLAS 1:63,360 – 1" TO 1 MILE ROADS, RAILWAYS AND PATHS

M1	Motorway
	Motorway Main road under construction
A 6(T)	Trunk Road
A 623	Main Road } Single & Dual Carriageway
B 6465	Secondary Road
	Narrow Road with passing places
	Road generally over 4m wide
	Road generally under 4m wide
	Minor Road, Drive or Track
- - - - -	Path
→→→	Gradients: 20% (1 in 5) and steeper 14% (1 in 7) to 20% (1 in 5)
	Multiple or Single Track
	Narrow Gauge Track
	Bridges. Footbridge
	Tunnel Cutting
	Freight Line, Siding or Tramway
a b	Station (a) principal (b) closed to passengers
LC	Level crossing
	Viaduct Embankment

PUBLIC RIGHTS OF WAY

-·-·-·-·-	Road used as a Public Path
-·+·+·+·+·	By-way open to all traffic
··············	Footpath
- - - - -	Bridleway

Public rights of way indicated by these symbols have been derived from Definitive Maps as amended by later enactments or instruments held by Ordnance Survey on 1st October 1989 and are shown subject to the limitations imposed by the scale of mapping.

Later information may be obtained from the appropriate County Council.

The representation in this atlas of any other road track or path is no evidence of the existence of a right of way

Danger Area   MOD Ranges in the area. Danger! Observe warning notices

BOUNDARIES

Symbol	Description	Symbol	Description
+ — + — +	National	·—·—·—	County
	National Park	+ + +	District
NT	National Trust	NT always open / NT opening restricted	
FC	Forestry Commission	Pedestrians only – observe local signs	

GENERAL FEATURES

Symbol	Description	Symbol	Description
	Radio or TV mast	P	Post Office
		PH	Public House
	Church or Chapel { with tower / with spire / without tower or spire	MP	Mile Post
		MS	Mile Stone
		LDP	Long Distance Path
○	Chimney or Tower	CH	Club House
	Glasshouse	TH	Town Hall, Guildhall or equivalent
	Bus or Coach Station	PC	Public Convenience (in rural areas)
△	Triangulation Pillar	VILLA	Roman Castle Non-Roman
	Windmill	⚔	Battlefield (with date)
	Windpump	☆	Tumulus
		+	Site of Antiquity
	Electricity Transmission Line		
> — > — >	Pipe Line		Woods
	Quarry		Orchard
	Spoil Heap or Refuse Tip		Park or Ornamental Grounds

WATER FEATURES

Marsh or salting
Towpath   Lock
Aqueduct   Canal   Ford
Lake   Weir   Bridge   Normal tidal limit
Footbridge
Canal (dry)

HEIGHTS AND ROCK FEATURES

outcrop   cliff   600   650   scree

·144   Heights are to the nearest metre above mean sea level

Heights shown close to a triangulation pillar refer to the station height at ground level and not necessarily to the summit.

TOURS

2 🚗	Start point of tour		Featured tour
→	Direction of tour	⑥	Point of Interest

TOURIST INFORMATION

Symbol	Description	Symbol	Description
	Camp Site		Nature reserve
	Caravan Site	☆	Other tourist feature
	Information Centre		Preserved railway
P P	Parking Facilities		Racecourse
	Viewpoint		Wildlife park
	Picnic site		Museum
	Golf course or links		Nature or forest trail
	Castle		Ancient monument
	Cave		Places of interest
	Country park	((	Telephones : public or motoring organisations
	Garden	PC	Public Convenience
	Historic house	▲	Youth Hostel
⊕	**Mountain Rescue Post**		

◆ ◆◆ ◆   Waymarked Path / Long Distance Path / Recreational Path

78

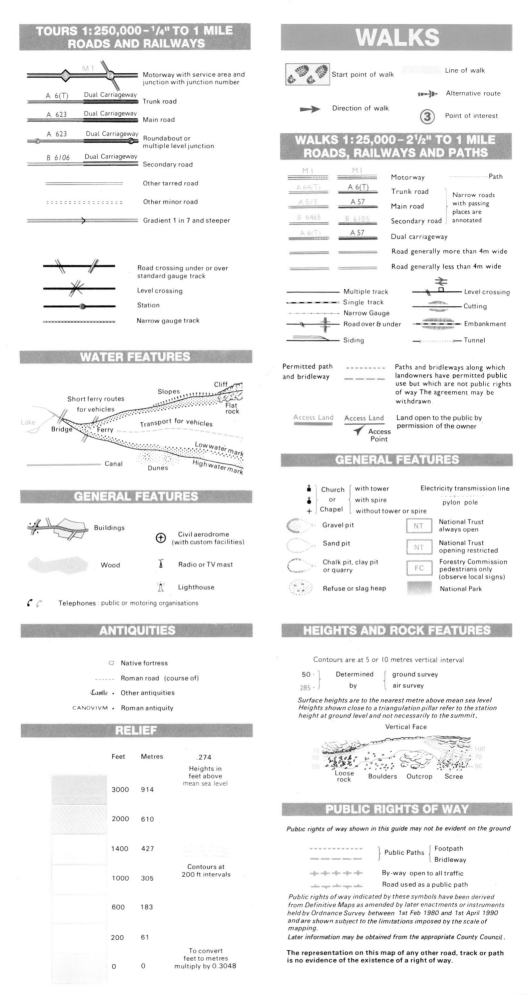

TOURS 1:250,000 – ¼" TO 1 MILE ROADS AND RAILWAYS

M 1	Motorway with service area and junction with junction number
A 6(T) Dual Carriageway	Trunk road
A 623 Dual Carriageway	Main road
A 623 Dual Carriageway	Roundabout or multiple level junction
B 6106 Dual Carriageway	Secondary road
	Other tarred road
	Other minor road
	Gradient 1 in 7 and steeper

	Road crossing under or over standard gauge track
	Level crossing
	Station
	Narrow gauge track

WATER FEATURES

Short ferry routes for vehicles
Slopes
Cliff
Flat rock
Lake
Bridge   Ferry   Transport for vehicles
Low water mark
Canal   Dunes   High water mark

GENERAL FEATURES

	Buildings	⊕	Civil aerodrome (with custom facilities)
	Wood	⟂	Radio or TV mast
		⟂	Lighthouse
((	Telephones : public or motoring organisations		

ANTIQUITIES

⸬	Native fortress
-------	Roman road (course of)
Castle •	Other antiquities
CANOVIVM •	Roman antiquity

RELIEF

Feet	Metres	
		.274 Heights in feet above mean sea level
3000	914	
2000	610	
1400	427	
1000	305	Contours at 200 ft intervals
600	183	
200	61	
0	0	To convert feet to metres multiply by 0.3048

WALKS

👣👣	Start point of walk		Line of walk
		▸■▸	Alternative route
➡	Direction of walk	③	Point of interest

WALKS 1:25,000 – 2½" TO 1 MILE ROADS, RAILWAYS AND PATHS

M I	M I	Motorway	.... Path
A 64(T)	A 6(T)	Trunk road	Narrow roads with passing places are annotated
A 515	A 57	Main road	
B 6465	B 6105	Secondary road	
A 6(T)	A 57	Dual carriageway	
		Road generally more than 4m wide	
		Road generally less than 4m wide	

	Multiple track		Level crossing
	Single track		Cutting
	Narrow Gauge		
	Road over & under		Embankment
	Siding		Tunnel

Permitted path and bridleway	- - - - - - - -	Paths and bridleways along which landowners have permitted public use but which are not public rights of way The agreement may be withdrawn.
Access Land	Access Land ⤶ Access Point	Land open to the public by permission of the owner

GENERAL FEATURES

♦	Church	with tower	Electricity transmission line
♦	or	with spire	pylon pole
+	Chapel	without tower or spire	
	Gravel pit		NT National Trust always open
	Sand pit		NT National Trust opening restricted
	Chalk pit, clay pit or quarry		FC Forestry Commission pedestrians only (observe local signs)
	Refuse or slag heap		National Park

HEIGHTS AND ROCK FEATURES

Contours are at 5 or 10 metres vertical interval

50 ·	Determined	ground survey
285 ·	by	air survey

Surface heights are to the nearest metre above mean sea level Heights shown close to a triangulation pillar refer to the station height at ground level and not necessarily to the summit.

Vertical Face

Loose rock   Boulders   Outcrop   Scree

PUBLIC RIGHTS OF WAY

Public rights of way shown in this guide may not be evident on the ground

- - - - - - - -	} Public Paths {	Footpath
		Bridleway
+-+-+-+-+-		By-way open to all traffic
-+-+-+-+-		Road used as a public path

Public rights of way indicated by these symbols have been derived from Definitive Maps as amended by later enactments or instruments held by Ordnance Survey between 1st Feb 1980 and 1st April 1990 and are shown subject to the limitations imposed by the scale of mapping.
Later information may be obtained from the appropriate County Council.

The representation on this map of any other road, track or path is no evidence of the existence of a right of way.

Key to Atlas pages

81

Distances in miles to BUXTON
Map Ref: 91 SK 0673

Birmingham	66	London	158
Bradford	54	Manchester	24
Chester	70	Nottingham	56
Leeds	58	Sheffield	29
Liverpool	55	Stoke-on-Trent	22

PEAK
DISTRICT

91

10

14

16

Colshaw Green, Summerhill, Leycote, Fough, Tor Rock, Cave, Dowall Hall, Hatch-a-Way, Jericho, Glutton Grange, Parkhouse Hill, Fernydale, Works, Street House Fm, Greatlow, Moor Lane, High Peak Trail

Tenterhill, Hollins Hill, Hollins Fm, Chrome Hill, Glutton Bridge, Earl Sterndale, Aldery Cliff, Abbotside, Wheeldon Trees, Hurdlow Town, Cronkston Low, Sparklow, Inn

Dun Cow's Grove, Moor Side, Moseley, Hollinsclough, Stannery, Nabend, Fox Hole Cave, High Wheeldon, Cronkston Grange, Cronkston Lodge

Thick Withins, Edgetop, Hollinsclough Moor, Coatestown, Tunstead, Underhill, Under the Hill, Crowdecote, High Needham, Pilsbury Castle Hills, Pilsbury Lodge, Mosey Low, Pilsbury

Smallshaw Fm, High Ash, Ball Bank House Fm, Hole Carr, Fawside Edge, Fawside, Marnshaw Head, Hardings Booth, Edgetop, Upper Whitle, Knowsley Cross, Motte & Baileys, Broadmeadow Hall, Cairn, Mines (dis)

Oakenclough Hall, Shining Ford, Hilend, The Lane, Fawfieldhead, Hallhill, School Clough, Waterhouse Fm, Brownspit, Over Boothlow, Lower Boothlow, Under Whitle, Top Fm, Race Ho, Carder Low

Newtown, Bank Ho, The Bent, Ridge Fm, The Ferns, Bridge End, The Low Ludburn, Fernyknowle, Ridge End, Hill End, Sheen Hill, High Sheen, Slate House, Harris Close, Mines (dis)

Boarsgrove, Round Knowl, Boosley Grange, Smedley Sytch, The Holmes, Pool Flat Head, Marsh Ho, Moorhouse, Sheen, Motte, Moat Hatt, Sprink, Bank Top

Folly, Oxbatch, Upper Fleet Green, Shawfield, Reaps Moor, Rewlach, Field Head, Hulme Ho, Brund, Fold Fm, Townend, Bridge-end, Factory

Lower Fleetgreen, Lum Edge, Swallow Moss, Hayes, Hayeshead, Wigginstall, Lowend, Scaldersitch, Banktop, Hole End, The Raikes, Hartington, Hotel, Crossl Sides

Upper Hay Corner, Averhill Side, Revidge, Steps, Clough Head, Warslow Hall, Weir, Hulme End, Weir, Tower, Upper Hurst, Lower Hurst, Dale, Cave

New York, Hob Hay, Royledge, Upper Elkstone, Cowhay Head, Townhead, Oils Heath, Warslow, Cowlow, West Side, Harecops, The Field Fm

Upper Green, Hill Ho, Ryecroft, Lower Elkstone, Heath Ho, The Lee, Ecton, Ecton Hill, Archford Moor, Narrowdale, Narrowdale Hill, Gratton Hill

Upper Acre, Manor Fm, Meadows, Hole, Stoneyfold, Brownlow, Heathy Roods, Tunnel, Swainsley, Back of Ecton, Top of Ecton, Paddock House, Gateham Grange, Gateham

Mixon, Mine (dis), Cave, The Hill, Brund Hays, Farmoor, Clayton, Ivy Ho, Kirksteads, Sugarloaf, Manor Ho, Tumuli

Newhouse Fm, Black Brook, Golden Hill, Bolland's Hall, Wallacre, Wettonmill Hill, Wetton, Butterton Moor, The Twist, Butterton, Coxen Green, Twistgreen, Waterslacks, Under Wetton, Steep Low, The Rakes, Pea Low, Alstonefield

Waterhouse, Butterton Moor End, Onecote Grange, Hall, Hillsdale, Cave, Ossoms Hill, Wetton Low, Hope Marsh, Hope, Hopedale

Onecote, Onecote Old Hall, Grindon Moor, Sheldon, Pen Fm, Grindonmoor Gate, Ladyside, Thors Cave, Elderbush Cave, Tumuli

Moorside, Bullclough, Clough Ho, Grindon, Weags Br, Beeston Tor Cave, Mines (dis), Stanshope, Long Low, Grove Fm, Dangate

Pewit Hall, Ford, Ford Wetley, Ryebrook, Mayfurlong, Deepdale Fm, Oldpark Hill, Manifold Track, Cheshire Wood, Weir, Castern, Hall, Beechenhil

Lark Park, Bottom House, Fair View Fm, Pethillshead, Ford Grange, Felthouse, Oldfields Fm, Soles Hill, Throwley Hall, Throwley Cottage, Steeplehouse Fm

STAFFORDSHIRE MOORLANDS DISTRICT, Martin's Low, New Street, Pethills, Waterfall Cross, Waterfall, Farwall, Mere Hill, Rushley, Musden Grange

Blakelow, Pelham, Blackbrook, Iron Pits, Back o' th' Brook, Cart Low, Slade Ho, Musden Wood, Musden Low, Ilam Country Park, Hinkley Wood

Rock Fm, The Moorlands Farm Park, Gutter Fm, Winkhill, Field House, Lamber Low, Calton, Doglane Fm, Upper Musden, The Waterings

Swineholes, Higher Parkhead, Birch Ho, Crowtrees, Waterhouses, Quarry (dis), Greensides, Calton Green, Hazelton Clump

Blakelow, Parknook, Black Heath, Broomyshaw, Stonyrock, Milk, The Waterings

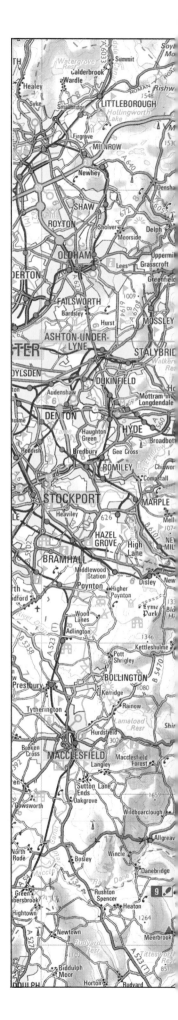

TOUR 1

HIGH PEAK PASSES

The highest and wildest moors of the Peak District are crossed by few roads, their names notorious from winter road reports. But for the motorist they offer a real taste of wilderness, less than 20 miles from the centres of Sheffield and Manchester.

ROUTE DIRECTIONS

The drive starts from the great steel city of Sheffield ①. Approx 51 miles.

Leave Sheffield on the A57, following signs to Glossop, past the University and Weston Park Museum. In about 3 miles, you reach open countryside. Follow the Rivelin valley, passing the Rivelin dams to your left and the escarpment of Rivelin Rocks to the right, before taking the long climb up to Hallam Moors.

In about 6 moorland miles, passing Moscar Lodge on the right, the road drops and crosses Cutthroat Bridge ② into the rocky, wooded gorge of Hordron Clough. You emerge at the Ladybower Inn. Cross the Ladybower reservoir ③ by the great Ashopton viaduct.

For the next 6 miles, follow the A57 as it ascends spectacular Snake Pass ④, passing the remote Snake Inn on the right after about 4 miles. At the summit (1,670ft), cross the Pennine Way ⑤ and then descend steeply for 3 miles, to enter Glossop.

At the traffic lights in the centre of Glossop ⑥, turn right past the station on the B6105 Devil's Elbow road, signposted to Crowden. In 2 miles, enter Longdendale via the sharp hairpin of the Devil's Elbow.

Pass above the Rhodeswood and Torside reservoirs ⑦ with the Torside National Park Information Centre on your right. Turn left to cross the wall of the Woodhead dam, emerging at a sharp junction on to the A628 Woodhead trunk road.

Turn right here and ascend the Woodhead Pass ⑧, crossing the Woodhead reservoir and the valley of the River Etherow. In 3 miles, cross Salter's Brook Bridge ⑨ and continue the long climb over the wild moorland scenery of Gallows Moss to pass the Dog and Partridge Inn on the right.

In 3 miles, turn right at the Flouch Inn on to the A616 (signposted to Sheffield) and enter Langsett ⑩. Passing the Underbank reservoir on your right, go through Stocksbridge and re-enter Sheffield via the valley of the River Don and Oughtibridge, passing Wharncliffe Crags and Woods ⑪ to the left.

POINTS OF INTEREST

① Sheffield has emerged from its history as the steel-making capital of Britain, to become the cultural and business centre for South Yorkshire. It is famous for its 'Golden Frame' of beautiful countryside, and for its fine museums and galleries, such as those in Weston Park.

② The body of a man was found by the old bridge here in 1587, with his throat cut. The present bridge dates from 1830.

③ The Ladybower reservoir is the largest and latest of three which have flooded the Upper Derwent valley to provide drinking water for the cities of the East Midlands. It was opened by King George VI in September 1945 and covered the depopulated villages of Derwent and Ashopton. The foundations of the latter lie beneath the Ashopton viaduct, crossed by the busy A57.

④ Thomas Telford built a turnpike road across desolate Snake Pass in 1821, but for much of its length the route follows the line of the Roman road of Doctor's Gate, which ran between forts at Glossop and Brough. The tall posts by the roadside mark the route for vehicles in snow.

⑤ The Pennine Way, opened in 1965, is Britain's toughest long-distance footpath, covering 250 miles. It runs up the backbone of England from Edale to Kirk Yetholm, just across the Scottish border. Here it crosses Featherbed Moss, heading north for Bleaklow.

⑥ Glossop is a busy little Pennine town, founded on the wealth of its cotton mills and the patronage of the Duke of Norfolk. Part of the town is still known as Howard Town, the Norfolk family name.

⑦ When the string of five reservoirs which flood the Longdendale valley were completed in 1875, they represented the largest man-made area of water in the world. They still supply the Manchester area with around 24 million gallons of water daily. Sailing takes place on Torside reservoir.

⑧ The Woodhead Pass is one of the busiest trans-Pennine road routes, formerly crossed by a railway line which went under the moors in the 3-mile-long Woodhead Tunnel, now used to carry high-voltage cables. The construction of the first tunnel in 1845 cost the lives of 28 navvies. They are buried in the tiny Woodhead Chapel above the Woodhead dam.

⑨ As the name suggests, Salter's Brook Bridge is on the route of an ancient packhorse saltway between Cheshire and Yorkshire.

⑩ Langsett (the name means 'long slope') is a small gritstone village dominated by its reservoir. Completed in 1904, it has a mock-Gothic valve tower modelled on the gateway of Lancaster Castle.

⑪ Wharncliffe Crags, a line of gritstone cliffs (known locally as 'edges'), were the scene of some of the earliest rock climbs by J W Puttrell. The extensive woods are threaded by delightful paths.

TOUR 2
MANSIONS ON THE WYE

The valley of the River Wye is thickly wooded and a haven for wildlife. The combination of trees, clear water and weathered stone attracted the Dukes of Rutland and Devonshire to build great houses here.

ROUTE DIRECTIONS

The drive starts from Bakewell ①.
Approx 40 miles.

Leave Bakewell on the A6, signposted to Matlock, and in nearly 2 miles reach the entrance to Haddon Hall ②.
Continue to Rowsley ③.
Pass the Peacock Inn and turn left on to the B6012, signposted to Baslow. Pass the edge of Beeley ④.
Cross the River Derwent and enter the park of Chatsworth House ⑤.
Leave Chatsworth Park and continue to Baslow. Leave by the A623, signposted to Stockport and Manchester. Follow the Derwent valley to Calver ⑥.
Meet traffic lights and turn left on to the B6001, signposted to Bakewell. Continue to Hassop for about 2 miles, and there branch right on to an unclassified road signposted to Great Longstone.
On reaching that village meet a T-junction and turn right, then continue through Little Longstone to reach the Monsal Head Hotel. Here turn right on to the B6465 Wardlow road, passing on the left a point which affords magnificent views of the great, horseshoe curve of Monsal Dale. Continue to Wardlow, and beyond that village turn left on to the A623, signposted to Stockport. In 1½

miles turn left again on to the B6049 and pass through the village of Tideswell ⑦.
Stay on the Buxton road and in 1 mile pass on the left the Tideswell picnic area, then descend into Miller's Dale. Pass beneath a railway viaduct and turn right on to an unclassified road signposted to Wormhill, then climb steeply with good views of Chee Dale to the left. Beyond the hamlet of Wormhill bear left, signposted to Peak Dale, and after a mile note, on the left, the extensive limestone workings of Great Rocks Dale.
Continue with the Buxton road and descend, then climb and after a mile keep left. After another mile turn left on to the A6 for Buxton ⑧.
Leave Buxton by the A6 Matlock road, following a winding course through the attractively wooded gorge of the River Wye. Later, climb out of the valley to reach the outskirts of Taddington, at 1,139ft above sea level, one of the highest villages in England. After a short stretch of dual-carriageway descend through wooded Taddington Dale, then 3 miles farther turn left on to an unclassified road signposted to Ashford village ⑨.
Turn right through the village, and at the end turn right again, following Matlock signs. Re-cross the River Wye and turn left on to the A6 for the return to Bakewell.

POINTS OF INTEREST

① Bakewell is a market town well known for the dessert known as Bakewell Pudding, said to have been accidentally developed by a cook in the Rutland Arms during the 19th century.
② Built by the Dukes of Rutland from the 12th to 17th centuries, Haddon Hall is everything a medieval manor house should be, having escaped the classical facelifts given to many similar buildings. Standing on a slope beside the Wye, it contains many rare survivals, such as the Tudor kitchens and a painted 16th-century ceiling of the Dining Room.
③ Most of Rowsley's graceful houses are owned by the Duke of Rutland. The Peacock, built in 1652 as a private house, became an inn around 1828 and was described shortly after as 'the beau ideal of an English country hostelry'.
④ Beeley is an estate village at the south end of Chatsworth Park, laid out by Paxton for the 6th Duke of Devonshire. Beside the inn a minor road climbs to heather-clad Beeley Moor, 1,200ft, where there are more than 30 prehistoric barrows and cairns.
⑤ Known unofficially as the 'Palace of The Peak', Chatsworth is as complete an example of the neo-classical style as Haddon is of the medieval. Built in the late 17th century, this great house of the Dukes of Devonshire stands in an extensive deer park landscaped in the 18th century by Capability Brown.
⑥ A good 18th-century bridge spans the River Derwent at Calver, which is overlooked by an austerely handsome Georgian cotton mill. This was Colditz Castle in the TV series *Colditz*.
⑦ The splendid cruciform church in Tideswell, often referred to as the 'Cathedral of the Peak', was built relatively quickly between 1300 and 1370, so, apart from the soaring Perpendicular tower, it is almost entirely in the Decorated style. The village is known for its well-dressing ceremonies.
⑧ The attractive spa resort of Buxton wears its lineage on its sleeve. It was known to the Romans and early royalty, and its fine range of 18th- and 19th-century buildings leaves no doubt as to when it achieved its greatest popularity.
⑨ Sheepwash Bridge in Ashford in the Water is the most picturesque of several that span the River Wye. Among the many mills here was one where the decorative limestone known as Ashford Black Marble used to be cut and polished. The village dresses six wells in an annual ceremony on Trinity Sunday or the first Sunday after.

TOUR 3
PEAK MINIATURES

Winding through the south-eastern corner of the Peak District National Park, this tour visits stone-built cottages and rocky valleys, relics of early industry, grand houses and great churches.

ROUTE DIRECTIONS

The drive starts from Matlock ①. Approx 51 miles.

From Matlock, follow the signs to Derby to leave the town by the A6, winding through a limestone gorge to the spa village of Matlock Bath ②.

Continue along the A6 to Cromford ③.

In the village turn right on to the A5012, signposted to Newhaven, then turn right again for a long climb through woodland on the Via Gellia. After 4 miles reach crossroads and turn right on to the B5056, signposted to Bakewell. Continue for 1¾ miles, then turn right on to an unclassified road signposted to Winster. Descend steeply into Winster ④.

Leave Winster by the Bakewell Road, then ½ mile farther turn right and rejoin the B5056. Follow an undulating course for 2¾ miles, then cross a river bridge and turn right. Almost a mile farther on turn left on to the A6, signposted to Buxton, and shortly pass the car park for Haddon Hall ⑤.

Continue along the A6 to Bakewell ⑥.

Leave Bakewell by King Street, signposted Monyash B5055. In almost ¾ mile turn left on to an unclassified road signposted to Youlgreave. At the next T-junction turn right and continue over higher ground for 1¾ miles before descending a 1-in-5 hill to cross the River Lathkill. Beyond the bridge take the next turning left to reach Youlgreave ⑦.

At the church turn right (no sign), and in ¾ mile bear right to Newhaven. After another ½ mile keep left, and in 2¾ miles pass on the left a turning into a picnic site. At the next T-junction turn right on to the A5012, then shortly turn left to join the A515.

Pass the Newhaven Hotel and after 6 miles, at crossroads, turn left on to an unclassified road signposted to Tissington. Drive to Tissington ⑧.

Return through the parkland, then turn left on to the A515 Ashbourne road and continue to Fenny Bentley. Continue past the village for ½ mile, then turn left on to the B5056 to Bakewell. After 2¾ miles turn right on to an unclassified road to Bradbourne. At the post office in Bradbourne village turn right, signposted to Carsington, and follow a pleasant byroad, narrow in places, for about 1¾ miles. Then turn left on to the B5035 Wirksworth road. After another 1¾ miles drive alongside the northern extremity of the new Carsington reservoir. Stay on the B5035 for a farther 1¼ miles, then turn right to Wirksworth (unclassified; light traffic only). On the left as you enter Wirksworth is the new National Stone Centre ⑨. Descend into Wirksworth ⑩.

In the town centre turn left, then immediately right, with the B5035 to Crich. Ascend on to higher ground, then follow a long descent into the Derwent valley with views across the Crich Stand, 940ft. At the foot of the descent turn right on to the A6, then cross the River Derwent and immediately go forward with the B3035. At Crich turn left at the village cross (unclassified) and follow signs to the Crich Tramway Museum ⑪.

Continue with the unclassified road to Holloway and turn right into Church Street, signposted to Riber. In ¾ mile go over crossroads into Riber Road. Follow that byroad for 1½ miles, meet a T-junction and turn left, then ¼ mile later keep left and pass on the right the turning to Riber Castle Wildlife Park ⑫.

Descend steeply through hairpin bends, and at the foot of the slope turn right. Later turn left on to the A615 for Matlock.

POINTS OF INTEREST

① Matlock is a collective name for a loose gathering of individual settlements that were welded together into a single spa resort in the 18th century.

② There's lots happening in Matlock Bath in and around the Pavilion by the Derwent, including the Peak District Mining Museum. The impressive heights of Abraham can be ascended by cable car.

③ Cromford was where Richard Arkwright built the first successful water-powered cotton mill in 1771. Many workers' cottages are here.

④ Winster has a charming 16th-century market hall and a number of 18th-century buildings. Lots of little alleyways, or 'ginnels', run off Main Street.

⑤ Magnificent Haddon Hall is noted in particular for its chapel, its long gallery and its great chamber. The terraced rose gardens are also delightful.

⑥ Bakewell is famous for Bakewell Pudding, which can still be bought in the town. Bakewell is full of good old buildings, many dating from around 1700.

⑦ A charming, extended linear village, Youlgreave has a church with a splendid Perpendicular tower and some rather grand Georgian houses.

⑧ Tissington is considered to be the most beautiful village in the National Park. The Norman church faces a splendid Jacobean manor house.

⑨ The National Stone Centre, created in a former quarry beside the High Peak Trail, tells the story of stone from its origins, through its production, to its uses.

⑩ Once a great lead town, Wirksworth has a splendid church in a charming circular mini-close. It contains the Peak's earliest Christian monument, a coffin-lid dating from the late 7th century.

⑪ The museum is sited in an old limestone quarry and visitors are carried to it in trams, past Edwardian street advertisements.

⑫ The Park is a Rare Breeds Survival Trust Centre where colonies of European Lynx live and other endangered species breed in natural surroundings.

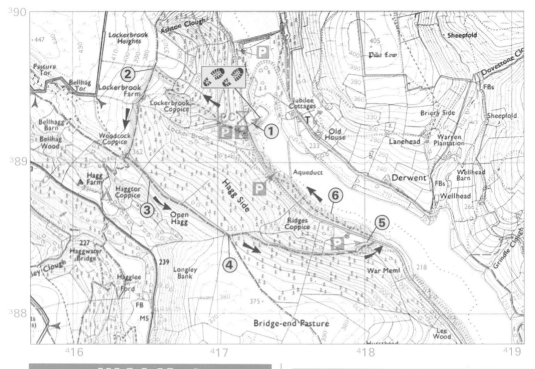

LADYBOWER RESERVOIR

Woodlands and water predominate on this walk in the Upper Derwent valley, sometimes known as the 'Lake District of the Peak' on account of its three big reservoirs: Howden, Derwent and Ladybower. Ridge-top vantage points offer splendid views of the reservoirs and the forestry plantations on their shores.

ROUTE DIRECTIONS

Approx 3 miles. Allow 1½ hours
Start from the car park along a tarmac road above the reservoir picnic area (grid ref. SK173893) ①.

Cross the main approach road, adjacent to Locker Brook, and follow a signpost direction up into the Forest Walk on a concessionary footpath.

Reach a 'leat' – which captures water from Upper Locker Brook for the Derwent reservoir – and cross this by means of a stile and footbridge. Continue ahead along a zig-zag path, with larch-stake steps at the steeper parts, keeping right at the junction with an exclusive path for the Lockerbrook Centre.

Continue through a broken wall and turn left to leave the plantation by a stile. Follow waymarks to a junction ②.

The main route turns left at the cross-tracks. Go through a gate and climb to another cross-track junction at the ridge top. Go left here and walk along the edge of the Open Hagg Plantation ③.

Continue along the high grass path to a stile and gate, where there is a signpost to Glossop and Derwent ④.

Descend the bridleway into a plantation and emerge from the trees at a gate. Continue down the 'Old Road' track and descend to the reservoir road beside Bridge End car park ⑤.

Go left and branch right along a concessionary path leading through the woodland between the reservoir and the road ⑥.

When you pass the pipeline, angle gradually up to the Derwent Overlook car park, then continue on a path alongside the road, slanting right and returning to the Fairholmes car park.

▲ Tranquil Ladybower reservoir, where valleys meet

POINTS OF INTEREST

① Fairholmes is a good base for exploring the popular Upper Derwent valley, being on a small promontory between the Derwent and Ladybower reservoirs. The car park has an information centre and facilities for cycle hire.

② A detour to the right at the cross-tracks leads to the shores of the Derwent reservoir at the foot of Ouzelden Clough. The Derwent was constructed between 1902 and 1916 – some 30 years before Ladybower reservoir.

③ From the ridge path along Open Hagg there are views west into the Woodlands valley. Through it flows the River Ashop, a tributary of the Derwent that feeds Ladybower reservoir. Upstream is the notorious Snake Pass, offering an exhilarating drive in fine weather but frequently closed by snow in winter. The valley is overlooked by the shadowy northern edges of Kinder Scout.

④ The signpost is a relic from the days before the village of Derwent was drowned, after Ladybower dam was built. The isolated community was one of two villages that were sacrificed in the project to provide drinking water for Derby, Nottingham, Leicester and Sheffield. Also lost were 17th-century Derwent Hall and Derwent's Parish Church of St John and St James.

⑤ Bridge End is so called because it was here, before the reservoir was created, that the old road crossed the River Derwent. Ahead, on the skyline of Derwent Edge, are the Wheel Stones – sometimes known as the Coach and Horses, because in profile they are said to resemble a coach in mad flight across the moor.

⑥ The woodlands beside the reservoir here are carpeted with bluebells in late spring. The ugly pipeline farther along relays water from the Derwent dam to the Ladybower treatment works.

WALK 2

CAVERNS AND A CASTLE

Castleton is a Peakland resort of the best kind – offering plenty of scenic variety, both above and below ground. Echoes of distant man-made history are heard at ruined Peveril Castle, while many fascinating geophysical secrets are revealed by close study of limestone bluffs that are effectively great fossil reefs.

ROUTE DIRECTIONS

Approx 5¼ miles. Allow 2½ hours
Start from Castleton's main car park (grid ref. SK149830).

From the car park's entrance go left into the village and turn right into Castle Street – where there is an information centre. Ahead is ruined Peveril Castle ①.

Go left across the Market Square to the unobtrusive entrance of Cave Dale, which is to the right, off Bargate ②.

The walk route continues along the dale and progresses through several metal gates. Cross a large pasture – passing a mere – and enter a small passage lane (note the sheep pens) to join Dirtlow Rake Lane. Turn right here, continue to where the lane widens and take the right-hand track along Rowter Lane ③.

Continue beyond the Rowter Farm access on to a metalled surface, reach a cattle grid and cross the B6061 to climb Windy Knoll before descending to the right ④.

A short, stiff climb from Windy Knoll leads to the summit of Mam Tor, **but care is required.** A stepped path which descends alongside the slippery scree to the

Blue John Mine and Treak Cliff Cavern makes an interesting addition to the walk ⑤.

This and the main walk meet at Winnats Head Farm. A minor road descends Winnats Pass from here to the Speedwell Cavern ⑥.

At Winnats go through a gate and keep right, following a track to reach Goosehill Bridge. Peak Cavern can be reached from the bridge along a narrow path running to the right ⑦.

Cross the bridge and follow the path downstream alongside Peakshole Water.

POINTS OF INTEREST

① Peveril Castle, begun in 1176 by Henry II, possibly on an Iron Age site, stands proudly on its still impressive natural bastion. The keep and part of the retaining wall remain. It was named after William de Peveril, who acted for Henry as forest bailiff.

② Cave Dale's tiny entrance leads into a beautiful secluded valley. Streams come and go along the dale – disappearing into the swallow holes typical of limestone country.

③ From Bradwell to Eldon Hill the upland is streaked with lead veins which have been exploited since at least Roman times. More recently many of the spoil heaps have been re-worked for fluorspar.

④ The limestone outcrop of Windy Knoll includes the Bone Cave, where excavations by Victorians uncovered the bones of bison, brown bear, reindeer and wolf.

⑤ Known as the 'Shivering Mountain' because its layers of soft shale are constantly crumbling, Mam Tor is crowned by an Iron Age fort. The Blue John and Treak Cliff caverns feature spectacular stalagmites and stalactites.

⑥ Speedwell Cavern at Winnats Pass is an old lead mine. It can be reached by a 104-step descent and a boat trip along an underground canal.

⑦ Peak Cavern, below Peveril Castle, is so huge that it once sheltered cottages. Peakshole Water, a tributary of the Derwent, emerges from its mouth. Tours are available.

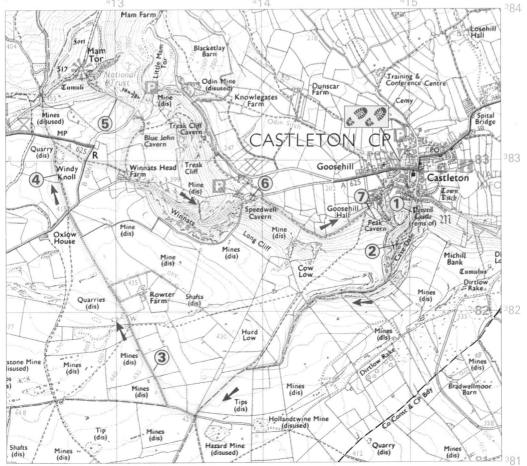

WALK 3

BRETTON AND ABNEY

Bretton, meaning the 'newly tilled land' is famous for its superbly situated pub, the Barrel Inn. Perched upon Eyam Edge it provides a marvellous southerly prospect across the limestone uplands, a landscape of drystone walls. The walk, however, turns northwards to explore the Derwent's isolated island of gritstone wherein flow two attractive streams through Abney and Bretton Cloughs: the latter is noted for its ancient landslips.

ROUTE DIRECTIONS

Approx 5 miles. Allow 2 hours
Start from broad verge at the sharp bend on Broad Low above Eyam Ridge (grid ref. SK210777).

Walk east along the straight, rough-tracked lane dipping and rising through the cutting between the summit of Sir William Hill ① and the radio masts. Descend to where ladder stiles mark the crossing of a footpath. Go left (north), through the heather over the Stanage ridge ②. Guided by waymark posts the path descends to the foot of the grouse moor, where the walls converge on the ridge.

Cross the stile and follow the track beside the wall, enjoying the notable view west up Bretton Clough. Cross a ladder stile. The track now meanders away from the wall, and from the vicinity of the crumbling barn, sweeping down to Stoke Ford ③. Cross the two plank footbridges with the stile between.

From the three-way footpath sign, go left, signposted to Abney. This path rises up to the delightful woodland track within Abney Clough. Above the woodland the path follows the hedgeline to a stile joining a track. This rises from the ford, and leads up to a decrepit gate, opening into Diddykirk Lane. The lane passes a farm tip in the clough head, and then rises to a gate on to the street in Abney.

Go left, passing the village hall and Top Cottage, to find the stile on the left, opposite Ash House Farm. Here there is a footpath signposted to Nether Bretton. Descend to the footbridge and mount the steps up the steep bank, with retaining boards, to the handgate. The footpath curves round the bank to cross a farm track. Walk diagonally to a stile in the corner of the field. Pass Cockey Farm via a gateway. Follow the farm track and where this turns sharp left through a gate, go right beside the wall, following it left to a ladder stile. Continue gently downhill through two enclosures. Go through a gate to reach a stile on the left, next to a spring flowing invitingly into a bath. Descend through the light birchwood. Cross a pair of plank footbridges, with a stile between, over Bretton Brook.

The path climbs the bank quite steeply to reach a stile with a fine view down Bretton Clough ④. Continue the ascent via a low stile. Following the wall, pass through a gateway rising to a footpath sign, and then angle left to a wall stile between the cottage and the ruin at Nether Bretton. Joining the road, either turn right to the Barrel Inn, concluding the walk panoramically along the Eyam Edge road, or take the peaceful green lane left, which passes round Bretton Moor to Broad Low.

POINTS OF INTEREST

① The rough-surfaced lane was constructed in 1757 as an integral part of the trans-Pennine Turnpike Trust system. Sir William Hill derives its name from Bess of Hardwick's grandson, Sir William Cavendish, who lived at Stoke Hall. He fought for the Royalist cause at Marston Moor in 1644.

② Right of the old quarry a large gritstone boulder is visible. On top of this resistant gritstone block is the Rock Basin. There are Bronze Age constructions on Eyam Moor.

③ Stoke Ford is a popular objective for ramblers. A Peak and Northern Counties Footpath Preservation Society signpost (No. 99) of 1939 still survives here. The landowner has erected a notice requesting visitors to refrain from building dams and leaving litter at this attractive watersmeet – please respect his wishes.

④ Bretton Clough is noted for its insecure slopes. The gritstone scarps are undermined by claybeds, which lubricate the rock and have caused it to slide into the clough. Hence the irregular slopes and shelves in this vicinity.

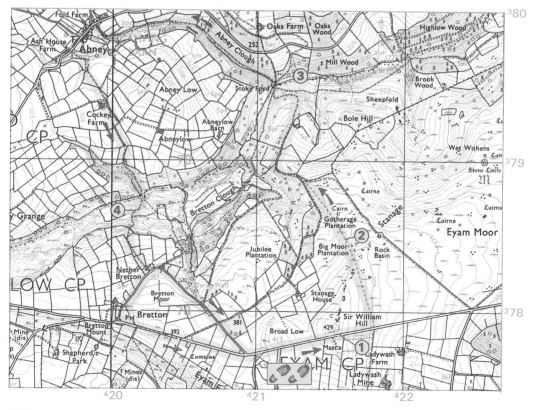

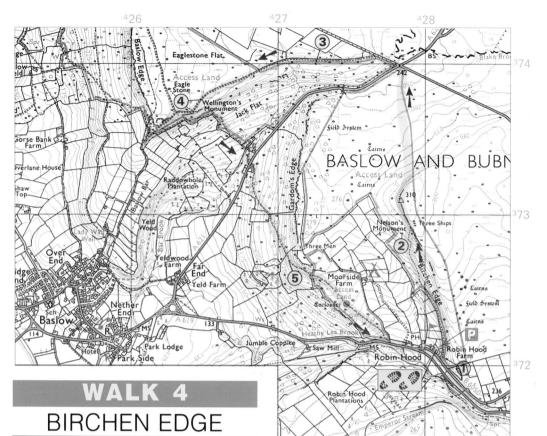

WALK 4
BIRCHEN EDGE

West from the conurbations of Sheffield and Chesterfield rises an upland slope, which becomes progressively wilder as it approaches the National Park boundary. It becomes broad moorland breaking into west-facing gritstone crags, providing abundant recreational opportunities for visitors from town and country alike.

ROUTE DIRECTIONS

Approx 4 miles. Allow 2¼ hours
Start from the Birchen Edge car park adjacent to the Robin Hood Inn (grid ref. SK281722).

A few yards east of the car park, cross the stile on the left of the B6050, signposted to Birchen Edge ①. Follow the clearly waymarked path through birchwood and boulders. For an easier walk you can take the early route to the right, or you can opt to follow the way of the majority, scrambling to the craggy brink close to the main outcrop. This is particularly popular during the evening, when young climbers swarm up the many short gritstone routes.

Pass Nelson's Monument and the Three Ships ②, following the edge beyond the now redundant OS triangulation column marking the 1,017ft summit. Look for the path slanting off the edge to join the principal path, running below the rocks. This heads due north over a wet moor of rough grass and light birch to arrive at a ladder stile, leading on to the minor road.

Go left with caution, crossing the busy A621 at the crossroads. Follow the minor road over Bar Brook bridge, which rises to a handgate on the left. This gives access to the old Chesterfield Road ③. Do not be perturbed by the notice warning of possible encounters with Longhorn bulls; all the cattle are correctly fenced in off the right-of-way. The track heads west along the edge of Eaglestone Flat passing the Wellington Monument ④. Continue downhill to the gave giving access to the lane. Do not enter. Instead, turn sharp left, beside the wall. Descend below the boulders and the oakwood scarp sweeping down Jack Flat. After crossing a stile go through a narrow passage to reach an old packhorse footbridge over Bar Brook.

Cross the A621 once more, keeping left of Cupola

Cottage via the stile. Ascend the clear path beneath Gardom's Edge. Pass through the third gap in the wall, where a diversion can be made to the Three Men of Gardom viewpoint up on the left ⑤. The main route continues by crossing over the shoulder of the hill, past the faint outline of a Bronze Age ring enclosure. Return to the A619 Chesterfield Road at a stile. Go left along the pavement, passing the Eric Byne Memorial Campsite, to conclude the walk.

POINTS OF INTEREST

① At the entrance to the Peak Park Eastern Moors Estate, a noticeboard defines the extensive open-access areas of the park and shows special sanctuary areas, where wildlife and historic monuments receive sensitive low-key management. The area is organised so that the public have liberty where they will gain most enjoyment, while at the same time the more delicate elements of this wild landscape can survive undisturbed.

② Next to Nelson's Monument, erected in 1810 by John Brightman of Baslow, stand three isolated boulders, the last traces of what was a deep gritstone rockbed, scoured away in the last Ice Age. The boulders, known collectively as the Three Ships, have been inscribed with the names *Royal Soverin* (sic), *Reliance* and *Victory*. They honour Nelson's successes at the Battles of the Nile (1798) and Trafalgar (1805), where he was mortally wounded.

③ Chesterfield Road. Beside this old way stands a stone marker, or stoop, from the days of horse traffic, when this was the main route into the Derwent valley from the east.

④ The 10ft-high obelisk was raised in 1816 to the memory of the Duke of Wellington, to correspond with the national hero commemorated on Birchens Edge. Some 200yds north-west is the Eagle Stone – the name is a corruption of 'eccles' and may signify that it was a place of early Christian gatherings.

⑤ Gardom's 'Three Men' are ancient cairns. They probably date from around 2000bc when the area was well populated and the focus of religious ceremonies: note the ring enclosure.

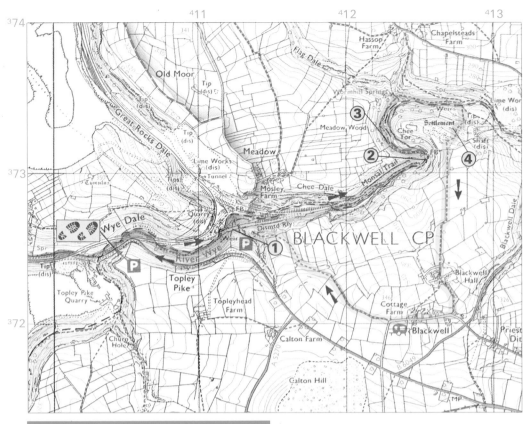

WALK 5
CHEE DALE

Beautiful as it is, this memorable Grand Canyon of a walk among woodlands, rock and tumbling water cannot be recommended to everybody. There are two eerie tunnels to pass through, some slippery rock steps and a precipitous finale requiring care to negotiate safely. However, the first part of the walk along railway trackbeds is easy and safe and can be undertaken by the young and old alike.

ROUTE DIRECTIONS

Approx 4½ miles. Allow 2½ hours
Start from Wye Dale car park on the A6 opposite Topley Pike Quarry (grid ref. SK103724).

Follow the riverside track running downstream through the woods. This is the haunt of fly-fishers – so quiet, please. Just prior to the third viaduct, climb the steps in the bank to the trackbed of the Monsal Trail ①.

Go left to read the information panel, before heading east through the impressive cutting, alongside the high crags, and across the Wye. Continue through two short tunnels to reach the closed entrance to Chee Tor Tunnel ②. It is suggested that young or infirm visitors turn back at the second tunnel, perhaps choosing to follow the riverside path for a variation.

Directed by signs, go right down a path to a footbridge. Cross it, before passing beneath the railway bridge. Descend to the water's edge, enjoying the fun of the Chee Steps ③ close to the overhanging rock wall. After negotiating the rough rock 'steps' above the river, cross two small footbridges to skirt Wormhill Springs.

After another rock step, approach the grassy bank, where there is a convergence of paths. Cross the footbridge and climb directly up the steep slope ahead, veering slightly right to a stone wall ④.

Cross this and the following wall using the stiles. Continue along the edge of an arable field beside the wall. Where the wall bears right, enter a gated lane leading through busy Blackwell Hall Farm. Descend the approach lane, passing the camping site on the right, to

the road.

Follow the street through Blackwell, passing Cottage Farm and a camping site. At the sharp left-hand bend in the road, go directly into the gated green lane, following it to its conclusion, then continue to a stile by the ruined barn. Head for a wall stile in the bottom left-hand corner of the pasture.

Walk along the foot of the next field to another stile leading to rough ground a few paces from the dangerous, unguarded brink of Plum Buttress. This is a notable viewpoint into Chee Dale and Great Rocks Dale.

Follow the path left. Take great care, as the path zig-zags down to a fence stile; avoid being lured down the ridge, which terminates with an arete. Go right, descending the side valley to a stile. Here the walk rejoins the Monsal Trail. Retrace your steps to Wye Dale car park.

POINTS OF INTEREST

① The Monsal Trail, linking Wye Dale and Haddon, is one of four footpaths that have been made out of former railway tracks in the Peak District. It became disused in 1968 and was eventually restored for use by walkers. Peak Rail has recently expressed an interest in restoring the old railway line.

② The trail runs up an embankment, passing the dramatic peak of Plum Buttress on the right, with its wavy bedding planes of carboniferous limestone. From here it is possible to follow an old footpath running down beside the River Wye. It meets up with the trail again at a footbridge below the blocked entrance to Chee Tor Tunnel.

③ In very wet weather the Chee Steps can be totally impassable, though this is uncommon. The wall of Chee Tor to the right, across the rushing waters of the River Wye, is worthy of notice. Wormhill Springs are the largest in the White Peak. Here, water gushes over a delta of rocks to charge the Wye with copious supplies of crystal water.

④ The settlement site is a fascinating survival from AD200. It is situated between the steep bank into Chee Dale and an area of cultivated land. Its intricate pattern of seemingly irregular rocky banks is evidence of a small farming community, thought to have existed here some 1,700 years ago.

WALK 6
BRUSHFIELD AND WATER-CUM-JOLLY DALE

John Ruskin, the Victorian art critic, struck out against the proposal to drive a railway through the beautifully wild Wye Dale sanctuary, 'so that every fool in Buxton can be at Bakewell in half an hour and every fool in Bakewell at Buxton; which you think a lucrative process of exchange'. His heart-felt sentiments brought no stay of execution. However, since the demise of the railway line nature has set to work, restoring it to its natural beauty, which was to Ruskin so precious. This refreshing walk gives expression to all the romance of the quiet uplands and the wild beauty of the craggy winding dale.

ROUTE DIRECTIONS

Approx 6 miles. Allow 2¾ hours
Start from the Monsal Head National Park pay and display car park (grid ref. SK185715).

Walk round to the Monsal Head viewpoint, leaving the road through the gap in the wall beyond Monsal View café. Descend right, but walk left as directed for the viaduct. Continue down through the scrub to the tunnel entrance. Cross the viaduct, taking the Brushfield path on the left and passing through the handgate. The bridleway climbs within an old lane, joining an unenclosed track. Continue above a mineral rake, noting the mine chimney below, to a lane overlooking Monsal Dale ①. At a squeeze stile next to a gate the valley view is lost. The track now follows a wall to a farther squeeze stile. Beyond this point there is no track. Continue as far as the three-way signpost (to Brushfield Hough on the left) and the gateway. Then join the track leading downhill to a gate.

Overlooking the steep woods of Taddington Dale, the track passes Lower Farm, Brushfield. At the junction at Middle Farm follow the road right and through a gate to Top Farm. Continue beyond Top Farm on the lane

above High Dale, which descends into a dip and then rises. Take the wall stile on the right. Walk up the pasture until reaching a wall stile at the top of the field. Pass through an old rake enclosure (following a worked-out lead seam, or 'rake'), to a fence stile. On entering the nature reserve, which is above some old mine workings, descend through light scrub to a stile. Do not cross the old railway bridge, but descend the steps on the right. Follow the trackbed for 30yds before turning left with the Monsal Trail. Go down the flights of steps and cross the Wye Mill stream, into Litton Mill ②.

Turn right, passing the shop, and go through the millyard on a concessionary path. Continue down Miller's Dale and Water-cum-Jolly Dale ③ to a kissing-gate at the millpond. Go right, crossing the footbridge in front of the weir. Go through a handgate and climb the steps on the left, to contour the slope above Cressbrook Mill ④. Join the trackbed once more at a handgate, where there is an information panel. Follow the old line past the former Monsal Dale station. After the cutting, approach the famous Monsal Dale viaduct. Turn left on the bridleway, down to the Wye footbridge. Follow the track round the back of the cottages and return uphill to the Monsal Head viewpoint and the National Park car park.

POINTS OF INTEREST

① The view over Monsal Dale features Hob's House landslip, beneath the prominent scarp of Fin Cop, and the Wye weir down in the valley. The hollows beside the track are evidence of lead-mining bell pits.
② The ghosts of orphans who were exploited as cheap labour during the early Industrial Revolution pervade Litton Mill. To gain a feeling of the working conditions of the times read *The Devil's Mill* by Walt Unsworth and *A Memoir of Robert Blinco*.
③ The concessionary path leading down Miller's Dale reveals a dramatic canopy of overhanging cliffs and trees beside the clear, fast-running waters of the Wye. On the third bend the waters become sedate as they enter the Cressbrook mill pond. The valley here bears the charming name of Water-cum-Jolly Dale.
④ Cressbrook Mill, currently used by a stone-dressing company, has a pleasing demeanour, a Georgian facade and a fine valley situation. The cotton mill regime operated here by Richard Arkwright was far more humane than many others in the early years of the Industrial Revolution. His lucky apprentices were fairly treated and even given a rudimentary education.

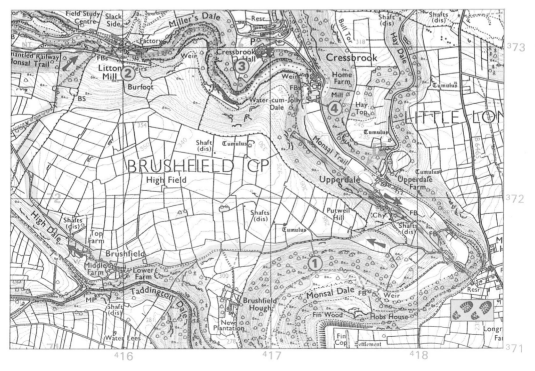

WALK 7
THE MAGPIE MINE

This walk ventures up the aptly named Deep Dale, with its briefly appearing stream, scrub woodland and ancient calcareous pasture. The walk continues through the attractive upland village of Sheldon and past the Magpie Mine, before it returns downhill again, into the sylvan Wye valley.

ROUTE DIRECTIONS

Approx 4¾ miles. Allow 3 hours
Start from the White Lodge National Park picnic site
(grid ref. SK171706).

Cross the stile and follow the clear path leading south, entering the dry limestone ravine of Demon's Dell ①. Cross the low wall stile. Pass directly through the rocky passage ahead, and then zig-zag uphill to a blue bridleway sign. Turn right into Deep Dale. Pass over the col next to the outcrop, which looks rather like Peter's Stone in Cressbrookdale in outline.

On entering Deep Dale bear left, beside the wall. Here there is a surface stream, sinking furtively into the 'kletter' (limestone chippings through which water drains). As the dale curves it can be seen to dramatic effect. Pass through a gate joining a tractor track and continue up the bridleway within the dale. Look out for the wall stile on the left. At this point, on the right, notice a line of hollows rising gently up the slope, clear evidence of bell-pit lead-mining. The footpath climbs up a steep slope, out of Deep Dale. At the wall stile is the first view of the Magpie Mine. Follow the unusually tall wall through four gates before bearing left. Cross three wall stiles to join the minor road; note that the walls on the plateau are much whiter than those in the dale.

Go left to enter Sheldon. Follow the street downhill. Opposite the Hartington Memorial Hall branch right. Go through the footpath passage, left of Gregory's barn.

A series of wall stiles and tiny enclosures leads to a mere. Bear right to a gate, and ascend a pasture with the wall on the left to a lane which angles right and terminates. Go left at the squeeze stile, walking directly towards the Magpie Mine ②. Cross two more.

Leave the mine enclosure along the path leading north-east. It goes past the roofless dynamite shed and over rough ground to a low wall stile. Cross the field and go through an irregular quarried hollow, to reach a wooden stile on the right of a galvanised trough. Then, passing the prominent corner of the wall, enter a green lane at a gate. Descend to the minor road. There are pleasing views towards the village of Sheldon.

Go left and then right at the wall stile, signposted to Ashford. Walk downhill through a horse paddock. After passing the mini sewage works, cross two wall stiles to enter Little Shacklow Wood. At the foot of the valley enter Nettler Dale on a forestry track. Descend to a stile on the right, and continue walking down the pasture towards the River Wye. Just before the river bank is a path near a gate. Follow the path to the left, joining the track. Go behind the old mill buildings, following the mill stream, and then walk beside the river upstream, to Magpie Sough ③.

As the ponds come into view the path begins to ascend. At the footpath sign continue along White Lodge path, walking uphill into Great Shacklow Wood and on to a ledge path with tantalising views of Fin Cop and Monsal Dale. At the junction with the path from Sheldon, descend to return via Demon's Dell.

POINTS OF INTEREST

① Demon's Dell is a collapsed cave system, carved out by post-Ice Age meltwater; many thousands of years of permafrost once allowed a stream to flow through this dry ravine.
② The Magpie Mine has a Cornish-style chimney stack and engine house, a Captain's House, a winch and cage, and a dynamite cabin. The site exhibits four centuries of fruitful and traumatic mining activities. It is preserved by the Peak District Mines Historical Society and is highly evocative.
③ Magpie Sough is the drainage adit for the Magpie Mine. It is 575ft from the mine surface to sough level, and the mine was sunk 153ft farther down in search of lead deposits. This hazardous venture was fraught with the danger of flooding, hence the need for a horizontal shaft. Today it is hard to imagine the appalling working conditions of the lead miners.

WALK 8

MANNERS WOOD AND THE MONSAL TRAIL

This quiet walk winds through scarpland woods, high pastures, lanes and meadows to join the track-bed of the old Midland Railway, revitalised today as the Monsal Trail.

ROUTE DIRECTIONS

Approx 5 miles. Allow 2 hours
Start from Bakewell Old Station Yard (grid ref. SK223690).

Return to the station entrance and follow Station Road uphill to the left. Branch right on to the bridlepath opposite Elmhurst, passing through the golf course fairway along a sunken track. Entering the woodland, the path steepens to emerge on the road near Ballcross Farm. Turn directly right into the bridle lane. Go through a stile. At the end of the lane the bridleway continues as an unenclosed track on to the terrace of Moatless Plantation ①.

Leave the terrace with the track, by the tree trunk used as a horse-jump. Walk across the pasture to a stile near the pond. Bear south-east, towards a stile beside a tumulus. Continue to the ladder stile just beyond the prominent corner of the plantation, passing a farther tumulus. Follow the blue estate signs through the conifer plantation. Cross an open strip of land, where there are telegraph poles, and go through a gateway. Here there is a restricted view over Bakewell. The bridlepath follows the ridge wall ② for a short distance. It then drifts downhill to join a woodland track. Follow

it left and then branch right, walking downhill to the junction.

Go along the lane leading west, with its delightful receding view of Manners Wood scarp. At the next junction bear right beside Shadyside Plantation, descending to pass the entrance of Bowling Green Farm. Where the track goes right, continue within the confined path to a dilapidated bridlegate. Follow the metal park fence and cross two arable fields, passing through two handgates. Then walk downhill to join the access road to Haddon Park Farm.

Bear left round the tunnel entrance (there is no access to the trackbed), and continue beside the metal fence to the foot of the hill. Turn right through the bridlegate, traversing the pasture above the marsh. Guided by the bridleway sign, bear half right uphill to reach a stile. Go into the lane and follow it left into Coombs Road. Go straight across the road. Walk uphill beside Coombs Road viaduct and on to the railway trackbed ③. Follow the Monsal Trail north, back to Bakewell Station Yard.

POINTS OF INTEREST

① Moatless Plantation stands on a circular eminence overlooking Bakewell. The name, a corruption of *Motelowe*, was Saxon for 'meeting-place mound'. It suggests that the hill was a centre of local administration in ancient times.

② The ridge wall defines the boundary between Calton Pastures, within the Chatsworth Estate, and Manners Wood on the Rutland Estate. (Manners derives from the Rutland family name and is of Norman-French origin.) Haddon Hall, a genuine fortified manor of 1350, lies at the heart of an estate that, since the Norman Conquest, has been owned by only two families, the Vernons and the Manners.

③ Coombs Road viaduct is the eastern terminal of the Monsal Trail. This footpath was established by the Peak National Park following the closure of the Midland Railway, which ran above Bakewell, in 1968.

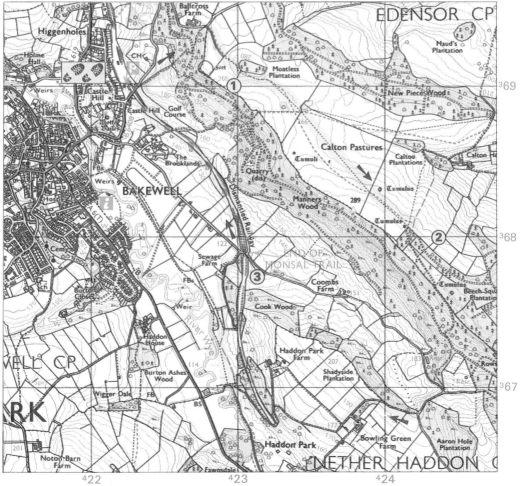

WALK 9
BACK FOREST

Walk along this delightful heather ridge to clamber through a secretive rock passage above the wooded Dane valley.

ROUTE DIRECTIONS

Approx 3¼ miles. Allow 1½ hours
Start at Roach End, where there is roadside parking (grid ref. SK996645).

From Roach End go west over successive wall stiles to accompany the ridge-top wall. Where it drops away on the left, continue along the ridge path through the depression ① to a stile, climbing on to the rocky crest.

▼The rock cleft known as Lud's Church (below) was used for Lollard meetings in the 14th century

Continue to a farther stile above a cleft. Descend to the track by the gate. Take the footpath to Danebridge, passing the welcome hostelry, the Ship Inn. Go right on to the track sweeping eastwards through the heather beside the forest boundary wall to enter the light birchwood at Castle Rocks. Here there is a fine viewpoint over Gradbach and the Dane valley. Where the path forks, go right, along the contouring path. This leads to a concealed entry on the right, into Lud's Church ②, via steps and a rocky passage. Pass through, climbing the steps. Take the right-hand fork at the far end. Walk to the last short flight of stone steps, and then follow the clearly evident firm path in the peaty soil left. Pass through the upper fringe of birch, heather and bilberry to a waymark post (concessionary to the ridge) ③. Go left for 30yds and then turn right by the pines. Keep to the path along the wooded brink. In 500yds descend to join the footpath emerging from Gradbach. Go right. The ascent is up a flight of rough stone steps close to the wall, rising to a squeeze stile. The stile gives access to Lower Roach End. From the track, complete the walk by turning right uphill.

POINTS OF INTEREST

① The Roaches Estate belongs to the Peak District National Park. The estate managers aim to encourage the co-existence of wild life and recreation. Rock-climbers' short-stay needs can be catered for, and walkers now have the pleasure of finding paths and walls restored, like those along the Back Forest ridge. Special concessionary paths have been created to give access to popular features, such as Lud's Church.
② Lud's Church is an intriguing rock crevasse formed by the lateral movement of gritstone, undermined by unstable clay beds. The high-sided cleft is safe to explore and compels the inquisitive walker's attention. It has been credited as being the legendary Green Chapel alluded to in the poem, *Sir Gawain and the Green Knight*. The poem describes their duel after an earlier clash at Camelot. Somewhat more credible is the local story that amid the ferns and mosses of this wet retreat the Lollards (followers of the religious reformer, John Wycliffe), held clandestine services during the reign of Richard II.
③ From Saxon up until early medieval times Back Forest formed the southern extremity of a vast red deer and wild boar chase, which became the Royal Forest of Macclesfield. This was upland hunting country administered by Ranulf and his heirs, the Earls of Chester, for the exclusive sport of kings and kindred noblemen. Under National Park stewardship the future of Back Forest is secured as a moorland sanctuary.

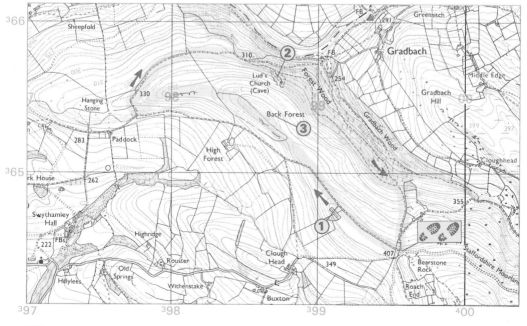

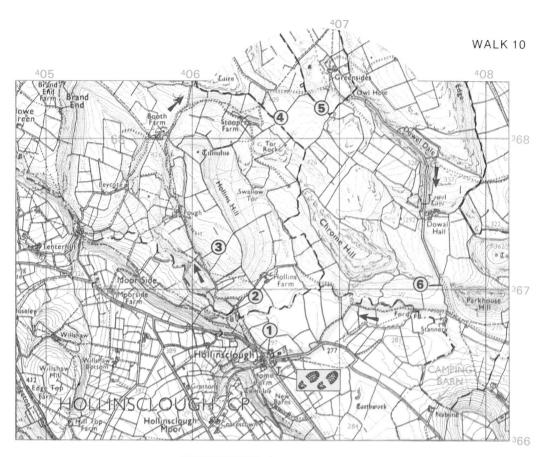

WALK 10

HOLLINSCLOUGH

The strong similarities with the mountain lime-stone scenery of the Yorkshire 'Three Peak' district lends this area an enhanced drama, made more spectacular by the limestone summits of Parkhouse and Chrome Hills, the only true mountain-like out-crops in the Peak District.

ROUTE DIRECTIONS

Approx 4 miles. Allow 2¼ hours
Start from the little village of Hollinsclough, parking near the telephone kiosk (grid ref. SK066665).

Walk north-west out of the village along the road leading uphill ①. After 200yds go right, through the bridgelate, descending initially beside a wall. Cross the River Dove over a packhorse footbridge ② adjacent to the Severn-Trent Water Authority flow gauge.
  Once through the heavy handgate, slant left, to follow the track uphill, through a gate and beside gorse banks. Enjoy the delightful views up the valley through Washgate Gorge to Axe Edge, the source of the Dove, Dane, Goyt and Wye ③. Pass behind Fough (pronounced 'fuff'), winding over the shoulder of Hollins Hill to a cattle grid. A sweeping right-hand curve takes the track away from Booth Farm, down on the left. Reach another cattle grid and branch right along the unenclosed track towards Stoop Farm. Follow the footpath sign and turn left, leaving the track. Traverse the pasture through a wall gap to join the track rising from Stoop Farm ④. Cross the cattle grid to reach the unenclosed minor road. Go right, keeping to the road. After passing several swallow holes ⑤, pass through a gate and after the tree-shrouded dump in Owl Hole, descend through Dowel Dale. Beyond the cattle grid at Dowel Farm and the Dowel resurgence, the unenclosed road runs beside Dowel Brook to leave the exciting amphitheatre created by the twin peaks of Chrome and Parkhouse Hills ⑥.
  Branch sharp right along the track that leaves the road, and cross the cattle grid flanked by stone gateposts topped by spheres. Head west to the ford and footbridge over the Dove. Continue beside the river to

join the metalled track from Hollins Farm. Follow this left to the cattle grid, and on to the Hollinsclough road. Turn right to finish the walk by passing the Frank Wheldon Centre.

POINTS OF INTEREST

① Hollinsclough, formerly known for its silk-weaving cottage industry, is a charming little community seen at its best when the daffodils are in full bloom; notice the Victorian postbox opposite the chapel. From here Chrome Hill's jagged spine has earned it the nickname 'the Dragon's Back'.
② The men who plied the packhorse routes across these inhospitable hills, 300 years ago and more, were known as 'jaggers', from the German for hunter. Their lifestyle would have been laborious and their train of ponies exposed to ambush as they conveyed valuable commodities like wool, silk and salt across the Pennines on regular routes, now marked by cobbled trails and packhorse bridges such as this one across the Dove. Other fine examples may be sought close by at Three Shires Head on the Dane, and just a mile upstream at Washgate.
③ Axe Edge, rising to more than 1,800ft in the north west, is a long gritstone escarpment which is often snow-covered well into spring. Its open moorland contrasts sharply with the verdant, tree-filled valley below.
④ The craggy summit of Chrome Hill, to the south, is a prominent landmark. It is one of a series of reef knolls – an isolated peak of harder limestone than the surrounding area.
⑤ The roadside is pitted with curious hollows known as 'swallets' or swallow-holes. They 'consume' moorland streams, which plunge through fissures to run their subterranean courses. They emerge, filtered cool and clear, at the foot of Dowel Dale from Dove Well; despite its name, this is not the source of the Dove, which rises on Axe Edge.
⑥ Neither Chrome nor Parkhouse Hills have rights-of-way traversing their summits. Their ecology cannot sustain recreational use, so visitors should refrain from venturing off the road. The pillar arete standing by Dowel Gap is known as the Sugar Loaf. There is a dramatic pass between 1,417ft Chrome Hill and the 1,221ft bulk of Parkhouse Hill. A secret place, it is worth any amount of walking to find.

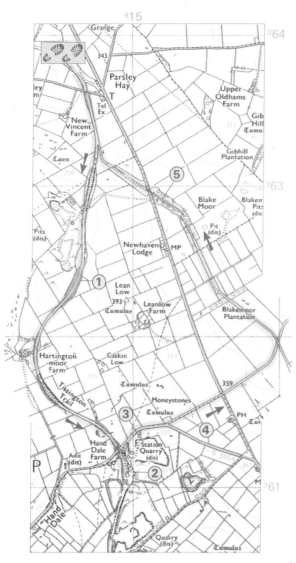

▼Once a railway line but now a long-distance footpath, Tissington Trail runs from Ashbourne to Buxton

WALK 11

PARSLEY HAY

The delightfully named Parsley Hay was the junction of two old railway lines that have found a new lease of life as much-used walking and cycling trails through the White Peak. Here there is a gentle circuit through the green landscapes of the plateau, setting out along the Tissington Trail and then following a green lane to pick up the High Peak Trail for the return. The walking is consistently easy, but watch out for the silent approach of cyclists. A shoulder-mounted wing mirror would be an asset!

ROUTE DIRECTIONS

Approx 4½ miles. Allow at least 1½ hours
Start from the Parsley Hay car park, picnic site and bicycle-hire centre (grid ref. SK147637)

Walk south for a short distance along the High Peak Trail, then fork right along the Tissington Trail to enter the impressive Parsley Hay Cutting. Continue to the second cutting ①.

Pass along a fine embankment section and, after Hartingtonmoor Farm, enter a third cutting before crossing the Hand Dale viaduct to enter the former station yard at Hartington ②.

From the station yard go left, down the approach road to join the B5054. At the junction turn right to pass the abandoned lime kiln ③. Continue for a short way on the verge, then cross the road and fork left into the broad green lane ④. Cross the busy A515 just 200yds short of the Jug and Glass pub and continue along the rough track to its intersection with the High Peak Trail.

Turn left along the trackbed, flanked by heather banks. Pass through the thin strip of Blakemoor Plantation to enter a cutting with a sharp bend – typical of this trail. Pass beneath the A515 through Newhaven Tunnel ⑤, returning to the start.

POINTS OF INTEREST

① In the second cutting along the Tissington Trail, fossil enthusiasts may wish to pause to search the limestone face and fallen debris for brachiopods, crinoids and corals.

② The embankment section of the trackbed offers wide, open views across Long Dale westwards to the hill of Carder Low (1,100ft). Hartington's former station, 1 mile north-east of the village, is now a picnic site. The signal box has been retained as an information centre. Mount the flight of steps to the former control floor, try your hand at cranking the levers, or glance at the pictures of the station in its heyday.

③ Stone 'beehive-type' lime kilns, often built into the hillside, like this one, were used to burn limestone. The soluble calcium was released in a powder form, for building or agricultural purposes; when applied to acid land it sweetened the soil, greatly enhancing crop productivity.

④ The tide of change has swept across this plateau since the Enclosure Act, with the introduction of predominantly straight walling. However, traces of burial mounds hint at ancient settlements, among them Money Stones. The green, rough-tracked lane was formerly the main cross-ridge route between Hartington and Middleton.

⑤ Upon each parapet of the Newhaven Tunnel (beneath the A515 road bridge) are original Cromford and High Peak Railway Company plaques, dated 1825 – the year in which the building of the line was approved by Parliament. The northern face is the more elaborate, bearing the Latin motto *Divina Palladis Arte* and the names of principal engineer Josiah Jessop and company clerk William Brittlebank.

▲ Main Street in the village of Elton

· WALK 12

ROBIN HOOD'S STRIDE

A gentle gritstone stroll on an old trackway, this walk visits two contrasting outcrops and a stone circle, before heading through woods and pasture back to the old mining village of Elton.

ROUTE DIRECTIONS

Approx 3¾ miles. Allow 1½ hours
Start from Elton's Main Street (grid ref. SK223609).

Walk west along Main Street. Opposite the Duke of York public house enter the churchyard, passing to the right of All Saints' Church ①. Go through the squeeze stile and across the access lane to a fence stile, close to a tank on the bungalow wall. Traverse the pasture (beware of silage effluent) to the signposted gateway. Continue uphill through the shallow combe, to a squeeze stile to the right of a line of ash trees. Follow the scarp edge a short distance before turning downhill on a narrow path. Cross a broken fence stile on your way to the stile into Dudwood Lane.

Go down Dudwood Lane ②. At the bottom cross the stile beside the gate. Go uphill to the Cratcliffe Cottage track and continue beside the left wall. Where the track veers right, ascend to the passage between Robin Hood's Stride and the larch plantation ③. Proceeding over stiles, cross the next two pastures diagonally passing the Stone Circle ④. Join the minor road opposite the entrance to Harthill Moor Farm. Follow the Limestone Way sign. Go right down the road, but shortly after the gradient steepens bear left by the Limestone Way sign, on to a very pleasant woodland path.

Emerging at a stile, cross it and walk through the pasture to another stile. Then bear left, leaving the Limestone Way. The creation of Matlock Rotary Club, it runs to Castleton.

Ascend the track, and go through a gateway where the tractor track bears left. Continue uphill to a squeeze stile beside a wall junction. Go uphill, following the power lines towards Tomlinson Wood, and pass through the squeeze stile. Walk round the plantation, before bearing half right to reach another squeeze stile. Go due south to a wall stile and cross the access lane to Cliff Farm.

From the succeeding wall stile, bear half left to another stile. Walk down the bank, over two more stiles, and on to the road. Go directly across to the squeeze stile, where a footpath is signposted to Elton. The stiled footpath leads into pastures and then rises beside a tall hedge. Enter Well Street through the gate on the left ⑤. Complete the walk by returning to Main Street.

POINTS OF INTEREST

① All Saints' Church once had a unique font. Complete with inverted salamander and a projecting stoupe, it was discarded in 1812 when the church underwent major rebuilding. Twenty years later the vicar of Youlgreave spotted it cast aside in the churchyard, and claimed it. For all the remonstrations of parishioners, it was henceforward lost to Elton. The present font is a facsimile of the original.

② Dudwood Lane lies on a Portway, meaning 'market road'. Probably of ancient origin, the Portway can be traced entering the Peak District in the vicinity of Belper, running towards Bakewell.

③ Robin Hood's Stride is a prominent outcrop of gritstone; despite its name, its Weasel and Inaccessible Pinnacles are too far apart for even this legendary hero to leap. Viewed from Elton it has gained the alternative name 'Mock Beggar's Hall'.

④ Nine Stones, robbed by wall-builders over the centuries, are relics of Bronze Age culture. There are now only four stones surviving.

⑤ Pay a visit to Elton's village shop, which conveniently doubles as a National Park information point.

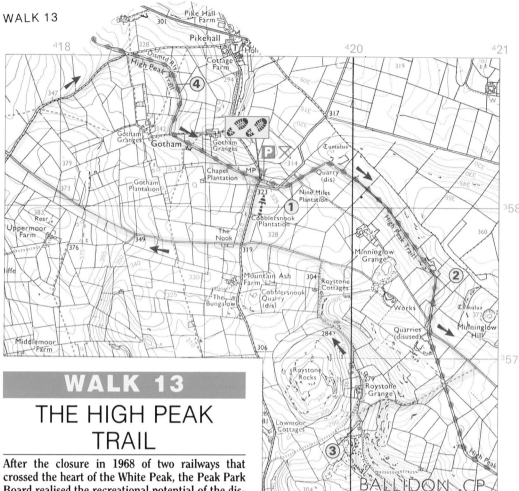

THE HIGH PEAK TRAIL

After the closure in 1968 of two railways that crossed the heart of the White Peak, the Peak Park Board realised the recreational potential of the disused trackbeds and turned them into long-distance trails for walkers, horse-riders and cyclists. About half of this walk follows a section of the High Peak Trail. The remaining half follows part of the Roystone Grange Archaeological Trail.

ROUTE DIRECTIONS

Approx 5¾ miles. Allow 2½ hours
Start from Minninglow car park near Pikehall, by a railway bridge over which the Cromford and High Peak line once ran (grid ref. SK195582).

Begin by walking to the farthest end of the car park from the entrance and follow 'Roystone Grange Trail' signposts ①.

Follow the trackbed round towards a large stone railway embankment below Minninglow Hill, passing quarry workings on the left and Minninglow Grange to the right ②.

After the lime kiln meet a gate bearing a yellow waymark superimposed by a black 'R', blocking the trackbed next to a National Park signpost. Cross this and note on the left another gate, also with a yellow mark bearing a black 'R'. This is the way the walk continues (the inviting gate and track diagonally opposite on the right should be ignored).

Turn left to cross the waymarked gate and a wall stile into Gallowlow Lane. Ascend past two fields on the right. At the third follow waymarks to Trail Bridge.

On emerging from the Trail Bridge continue downhill through pasture to an end wall near the field's bottom left corner. Cross this by a stile and follow the wall on the left through fields and over stiles to a farm track ③.

The main route is continued by turning right where the cross-country path meets the farm track, and runs through the farmyard of the present Roystone Grange.

Continue through gates, past Roystone Cottages, then meet Minninglow Lane and turn left.

Continue to Cobblersnock crossways, where a choice of routes may be made. By turning right alongside

Cobblersnock Plantation the metalled lane may be followed back to the car park.

A longer alternative is straight ahead at the crossways to follow Cobblersnock Lane past The Nook cottage and up on to Upper Mor. In just under ½ mile keep right at a fork in the lane and later continue straight on to the lane at the intersection of two ancient packhorse ways.

Turn right and follow Green Lane to rejoin the High Peak Trail after less than a mile. The walk is concluded by following the trackbed to the right round the Gotham Curve and back to the start ④.

POINTS OF INTEREST

① Opened in 1830–31, the Cromford and High Peak Railway was the first to link east with west across the Pennines – from Cromford to Whaley Bridge. Although it enabled coal, stone and other minerals to be transported much more easily in a remote area, the line was not a great financial success. Now the old trackbed has found a new use, and the 17-mile High Peak Trail is immensely popular.

② Relics of past industry survive along the course of the old railway. There are numerous quarries as well as workings to extract silica sand, and brickworks where this was used. Just past Minninglow Grange is the stone beehive shape of an old lime kiln. Much earlier settlers knew Minninglow Hill: this prominent landmark is crowned by a large neolithic burial mound, dating from about 2,000BC.

③ A left turn along the track offers a short detour to see the remains of a medieval farmstead – the predecessor of 18th-century Roystone Grange, just to the north. The ruined buildings were owned by a Cistercian abbey in Leicestershire, and include a dairy that has been excavated. Evidence of even earlier farming can be seen on the hillside nearby, where a Roman field system has been discovered.

④ In its day the Gotham Curve, which turns through 80 degrees, was the tightest bend on any railway in Britain. Only short-wheelbase locomotives and rolling stock could use it.

WALK 14

THROWLEY AND THE HAMPS VALLEY

This journey through limestone country contrasts some of the most dramatic valley scenery that the White Peak has to offer with an Elizabethan Old Hall and a water-silent valley, alive with the joyous sounds of birds.

ROUTE DIRECTIONS

Approx 5¼ miles. Allow 2½ hours
Start from Weag's Bridge National Park car park (grid ref. SK100543).

Walk south on the Manifold Track, leaving the trail at the beginning of the curve into the Hamps valley. Cross a stile on the left to join the access road to Beeston Tor Farm ①. The bridleway ascends above the farm with fine views of Beeston Tor. After the lane gate there are pleasing views down the Manifold valley ②.

The track winds uphill, passing a barn to reach a stile. Beyond is the natural and popular route, adopted by bridleway and footpath users, which follows the valley to the right of the strip lynchets ③. Climb to a footpath sign at the wall corner and bear left, rounding the wall of a bedraggled plantation to reach a stile. Descend to Throwley Hall ④. Find a stile to the left of the plantation and carefully pass between the water and cattle sheds to the farmyard and road.

Turn right and follow the minor road uphill, which becomes unenclosed beyond the cattle grid. Cross Mere Hill ridge and the head of Soles Hollow, with its large walled mere. There is a cattle grid after the access track

to Throwleymoor Farm. A stile goes right into the pasture which is immediately to the left of the lane to Woodhead Farm.

Descend to a stile and walk into the shallow, scrubby side valley, where a thin path leads unerringly down to join a rough track. This leads past Lee House to a sturdy footbridge on to the Manifold Track. Go right, down the normally dry Hamps valley, to complete the loop back into the Manifold valley.

POINTS OF INTEREST

① Ignore the path to the left, beyond the normally dry Hamps confluence, with access to Manifold stepping-stones and a climbers' approach to Beeston Tor. At the foot of this fine crag lies St Bertram's cave, where in 1934 a hoard of Saxon coins was discovered, together with evidence of Iron Age and Romano-British occupation. The finds were deposited in the museum at Buxton, as well as the British Museum. Jackdaw's Hole, the high cleft on the rockface, can be reached by climbers via a 30ft rift chimney from St Bertram's Cave.

② The name Manifold means precisely that: many folds, or winding valley. The river percolates into its bed at Wettonmill during the drier months of the year. It emerges at the Boil Hole beneath Ilam Hall.

③ Almost the entire slope to the left of the valley path is stepped with strip lynchets, the most complete exhibition of cultivation terraces one is likely to witness anywhere.

④ Throwley means 'trough-shaped valley'. Adjacent to the 19th-century farmstead stand the ruins of Old Hall, built in 1603 by Sampson Meverell to replace an earlier dwelling. The Elizabethan mansion comprised a two-storey wing, attached to a tower one floor higher. The scene is rather like one of time stood still, and the whole farmstead reflects many centuries of stock farming practice.

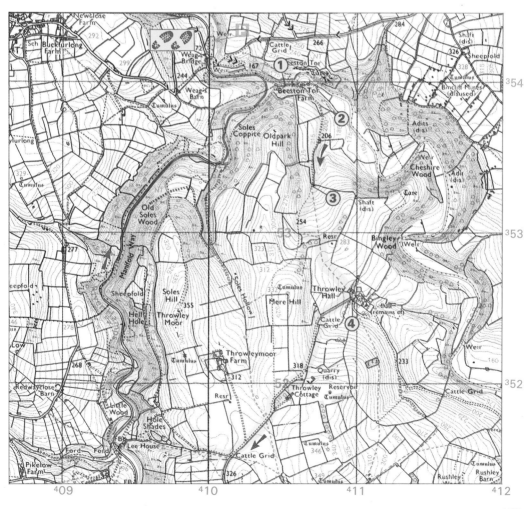

WALK 15

TISSINGTON TRAIL

Along the line? Down the track? Either way the Tissington Trail provides not merely easy walking, but good viewing across a typically beautiful White Peak landscape of verdant pastures and gleaming walls. The walk loops back over quiet pastures to pass through the charming little estate village of Tissington.

ROUTE DIRECTIONS

Approx 2¾ miles. Allow 1¼ hours
Start from Tissington Old Station (grid ref. SK178521).

Walk north on the Tissington Trail trackbed ①. The only hazard is the silent approach of bicycles from the

▲ Tissington is known for its pond and stone cottages

rear! On the way, pass under two farm bridges linked by a footpath to the trail. Following Crakelow Cutting reach the third footpath crossing point. Go left, signposted to Tissington, at a stile, ascending the shallow valley beside the wall. Continue by the wall to the second short lane, where there is a rebuilt wall to the right. Go over the ridge to a gate. Proceed downhill along a track, passing a mere ②. At a gateway, continue to the gate into a lane leading on to the road. Go south down the village street, passing on the west side Tissington Hall ③. Opposite the hall is the hall well, the central one of five in the village ④. At the foot of the street bear left, passing the village pond, to return to the Old Station car park.

POINTS OF INTEREST

① There is an information centre and toilet block at Tissington station. Further north, the two trail cuttings passed on the walk are managed nature reserves, so admire and respect the typical plantlife of these leached limestone soils. Many visitors mean many prying hands and sniffing dogs to jeopardise the delicate wildlife – so walk quietly.

② Notice the strongly emphasised, reversed 's'-ridge and furrows overlaid in this pasture, the distinctive product of oxen-ploughing. In order to efficiently turn the oxen plough-team at the end of each furlong it is necessary to begin the sweep round during the final 20 yards of actual ploughing. Draught horses can turn on the proverbial tanner.

③ Tissington Hall, a Jacobean mansion built in 1609, replaced an earlier mansion set on the so-called Seigework, in the pasture adjacent to the church opposite. It is the ancestral home of the Fitzherberts, whose monuments lavishly adorn St Mary's Church. The church's Norman tower is the most appealing element in an otherwise heavily over-Normanised Victorian restoration.

④ The village of Tissington is renowned for marking Ascension Day with traditional well-dressings. This custom originated in pre-Christian times. It can be witnessed in other White Peak villages, where water supplies are prone to dry up during summer months. However, within living memory the water has not ceased to flow in Tissington. Well-dressing continues to symbolise life in all its abundance – visit, in turn, Hand, Town, Hall, Yew Tree and Coffin Wells.

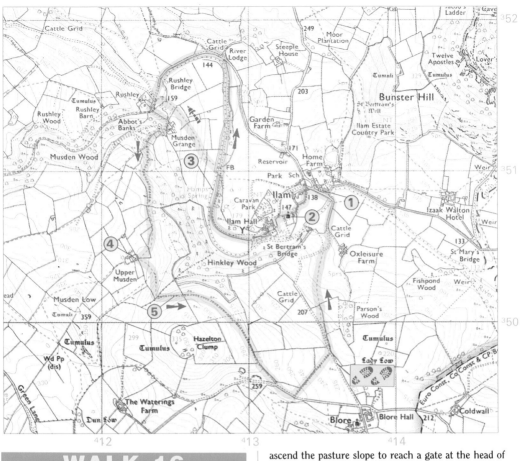

WALK 16

ILAM

The beautiful sweeping landscape of the lower Manifold valley forms the backdrop to this walk. The stage is set by appraising the hills that form the dramatic beginnings of the National Park. Descending to follow the Manifold through Ilam Park, the walk climbs above Musden Grange, returning along a bridleway to Blore Pastures.

ROUTE DIRECTIONS

Approx 4 miles. Allow 2½ hours
Start from the National Park Blore Plastures car park and picnic site (grid ref. SK136497).

Walk north from the car park, descending via stiles over pasture to the unenclosed road. Turn right to a cattle grid, and enter Ilam over Ilam Bridge. Go straight ahead into the village ①. At the entrance to Ilam Hall fork left along the drive to Dove House. Turn left at the gates to follow a path to the church ②.

The route continues either by descending steps to join the Paradise Walk near St Bertram's Bridge, or by crossing the terraced gardens, passing the Manifold Restaurant before slanting down towards the river. Either way, the Paradise Walk is joined and followed through the Manifold meadows and past the Battle Cross (read the plaque) to a footbridge ③.

Either cross the footbridge, climbing directly to Rushley or Musden Grange via a stile, or continue along the river to River Lodge (there is a private path across the garden).

Once on the road, go left along the river to Rushley Bridge. Cross it, ascending the track through Rushley Farm, and then bearing left to Musden Grange. Keep right of the farm buildings. Where the track switches right, slant left by an ascending wall. Go through a hedge gap above a small, tree-filled enclosure, and

ascend the pasture slope to reach a gate at the head of a shallow side valley of Hinkley Wood.

Follow the wall uphill to a stile crossing a pasture. Enter Upper Musden farmstead via a stile close to the barn ④. Go immediately left over the stile on the left, passing through open pasture beside an old hedgeline to a gate. The horse-jump betrays the odd fact that the path has been mysteriously upgraded at this point to a bridleway! Continue above Hinkley Wood ⑤. Go through farther gates to reach the minor road. Turn left, branching left after 150yds to a stile. Descend the ridge-and-furrow pasture to return to the car park.

POINTS OF INTEREST

① One of only two villages in the narrow Manifold valley, Ilam (humorously known as 11am) was moved in the 19th century. This was part of the grand design of shipping magnate Jesse Watts-Russell, who had Ilam Hall rebuilt to rival nearby Alton Towers. The village has a collection of tile-hung, bargeboarded cottages.
② An ancient building with a distinctive saddleback tower, Ilam church was massively restored in the mid-19th century. It has two fine chapels, as well as two Saxon churchyard crosses. Nearby Ilam Hall, rebuilt in Tudor Gothic style in the 1820s, was rescued from demolition in 1934 and given to the National Trust. The hall itself is not open to the public, but its 84 acres of lovely parkland are managed as a country park which is open all year.
③ During dry weather, the River Manifold sinks into its limestone bed several miles upstream at Wettonmill, to reappear in the Boil Hole directly below the hall at the beginning of Paradise Walk. Its tributary, the Hamps, whose name means 'summer dry', does the same percolating trick at Waterfall. It re-emerges across the meadow from Paradise Walk, having travelled surreptitiously beneath Musden Low.
④ Built in 1821 when the high pastures of Musden Grange were enclosed, Upper Musden farmstead has been derelict for several decades but has a ghostly charm with its crumbling walls and cobbled yard.
⑤ Hinkley Wood is a Site of Special Scientific Interest.

Page numbers in bold type indicate main entries.

A

	page
Abney	104
Agden reservoir	38
Allgreave	67
Alport-by-Youlgreave	22, 44, 69
Alsop en le Dale	60
Alstonefield	32
Alton Towers	70
angling	72
Arbor Low	7, 32
Arkwright, Richard	44, 107
Ashbourne	32–3
Ashford in the Water	25, 33, 44, 98
Ashopton viaduct	96
Ashover	22, 26, 34
Ashwood Dale	58
Axe Edge	16, 34–5, 111
Axe Edge Moor	34

B

	page
Back Forest	110
Back o' th' Brook	53
Bagshawe Cavern	22, 39, 70
Bakewell	8, 35, 70, 98, 100, 109
Bakewell puddings	35
Ballidon	8, 60
Bamford	36, 44
Baslow	25, 36, 98
Baslow Edge	36
Beeley	37, 98
Beeley Moor	37, 98
Beeston Tor	53, 115
Bentley Hill	65
Beresford Hall	32
Big Moor	36
Birchen Edge	105
Birchinlee	50
Birchover	37
Black Hill	65
Black Rocks	45
Bleaklow	15, 16
Blue John Cavern and Mine	34, 41, 70, 103
Bone Cave	103
Bonsall	37
Bottoms reservoir	65
Bow Stones	64
Bradbourne	8, 38, 100
Bradfield	38
Bradford Dale	69
Bradwell	8, 17, 22, 39, 70
Brassington	39
Bretton	48, 104
Brough	7, 39
Brushfield	107
Bugsworth Hall	41
Burbage	26
Butterley	43
Butterton	53
Buxton	8, 40, 70, 98
Buxton Spa	40–1
Buxworth	41

C

	page
Caldon Canal	53
Cales Dale	59
Calke Abbey and Park	70
Calver	26, 40, 44, 98
Calver Sough	40
Camphill	48
Carl Wark	55
Carsington reservoir	100
Castleton	22, 40–1, 70–1, 103
Cat and Fiddle Inn	35, 56
Cauldon Lowe	67
Cave Dale	103
Cavendish House Museum	71
Chapel-en-le-Frith	26, 41
Chatsworth House and Park	36, 42, 44, 71, 98
Cheddleton	53
Chee Dale	58, 98, 106
Chee Tor	8, 58, 106
Chee Tor Tunnel	106
Chelmorton	8, 42
Chesterfield	42–3, 71
Chestnut Centre	71
Chinley	41
Chrome Hill	111
Churchtown	45
Churnet valley	53
cinemas	75
Cocking Tor	34
Consall Ironworks	53
Coombes Edge	51
craft shops	75–6
Cratcliff Tor	46
Cressbrook	54–5
Cressbrook Dale	55
Cressbrook Mill	55, 107
Crich	43, 100
Crich Cliff	43
Crich Tramway Museum	22, 43, 100
Cromford	44–5, 71, 100
Cromford and High Peak Railway	9, 44–5, 48, 64, 112, 114
Cromford Mill	44, 71
Crowden Youth Hostel	65
Curbar	40
customs and events	23–6, 76
cycling	72

D

	page
Dale Dike reservoir	38
Damflask reservoir	38
Danebridge	67, 110
Dark Peak	6, 7, 15, 16, 46, 54, 66
Darley Dale	45
Deep Dale	108
Demon's Dell	108
Derwent reservoir	50, 102
Digley reservoir	51
Dinting Viaduct	48
Disley	71
Doctor's Gate	48
Dovedale	7, 32, 45, 58
drystone walls	66

E

	page
Eagle Stone	105
Earl Sterndale	55
Ecton	22
Edale	9, 44, 46
Eddisbury Park Field	56
Edensor	42
Eldon Hole	60
Elton	46–7, 113
Errwood reservoir	48
Eyam	8, 22, 26, 47
Eyam Moor	104

F

	page
Fairholmes	102
farming	66
Fenny Bentley	8, 65, 100
Fernilee	48, 64
Fieldhead	46
Fin Cop	56
Five Wells	64
Flagg	8, 26, 61
Flash	35
Flint Mill	71
fluorspar industry	34, 63
Foolow	48
Fritchley	43
Froggatt	40
Froghall Wharf	53

G

	page
Giant's Hole	60
Gib Hill	32
gliding	48
Glossop	48, 96
golf	72–3
Goyt valley	48
Gradbach	67, 110
Great Hucklow	48
Great Longstone	17, 56, 98
Great Rocks Dale	58, 69, 98, 106
Great Rowsley	61
Grin Low Wood	40
Grindleford	48–9
Grindlow	48
Grindon	53
Gulliver's Kingdom and Royal Cave	72

H

	page
Haddon Hall	49, 72, 98, 100, 109
Hallam Moors	96
Hamps valley	115
Harborough Rocks	7, 39
Harland Edge	37
Harthill Moor	46
Hartington	49, 112
Hassop	56, 98
Hathersage	26, 50–1
Hayfield	26, 51
Heights of Abraham	72, 100
Hen Cloud	53, 63
High Ordish	34
High Peak Junction Workshops	44, 71
High Peak Trail	14, 45, 60, 74, 112, 114
High Wheeldon	55
Hinkley Wood	117
Hob Hurst's house	37
Hollingworth Head	51
Hollinsclough	111
Holloway	100
Holme	51
Holmfirth	52
Hope	8, 52
Horton	61
Howden reservoir	50

I

	page
Ilam	25, 52–3, 117
Ilam Hall	52, 53, 117
information sources	74–5

K

	page
Kettleshulme	64
Kinder Downfall	46
Kinder Scout	11, 15, 16, 17, 46, 51

L	page
Ladybower reservoir	17, 50, 96, 102
landscape	6–9
Langsett	96
Lathkill Dale	7, 18
lead mining	19–22
Leawood Pump House	44
Leek	53, 71
Lin Dale	45
Little Hayfield	51
Little Hucklow	48
Little Longstone	56, 98
Little Rowsley	61
Litton	8, 54
Litton Mill	107
Longdendale	65, 96
Longnor	14, 55
Longshaw	55
Longstone	56
Longstone Edge	56
Lower Elkstone	67
Lud's Church	67, 110
Lyme Hall and Park	56, 71

M	page
Macclesfield	56, 71
Macclesfield Forest	56
Magpie Mine	19, 21, 22, 61, 108
Mam Tor (Shivering Mountain)	
	7, 16, 41, 103
Mandale Mine	21, 59
Manifold Track	74, 115
Manifold valley	7, 8, 53, 115, 117
Manners Wood	109
markets	75
Matlock	25, 56–7, 71–2, 100
Matlock Bath	22, 56–7, 72, 100
Meerbrook	22
Melandra Roman fort	7, 48
Meltham	57
Micrarium	40, 70
Middleton Dale	67
Middleton Top Engine House	68, 72
Middleton-by-Wirksworth	22, 68, 72
Middleton-by-Youlgreave	69
Midland Railway Centre	43
Mill Close Mine	22, 45
Milldale	32, 45, 60
Miller's Dale	58, 98
Millstone Edge	55
Minninglow Hill	7, 60, 114
Monsal Dale	56, 58, 98, 107
Monsal Trail	14, 18, 56, 58, 74, 106, 109
Monyash	14, 58–9
Morridge	55
Mottram-in-Longdendale	51

N	page
National Park Information Centre	46
National Park Rangers	27–30
National Stone Centre	68, 100
Nelson's Monument	36, 105
Nether Booth	46
Nether Bretton	104
Nether Haddon	59
New Mills	59, 72
Nine Ladies stone circle	62
North Lees	51
North Staffordshire Steam Railway	
Centre	53, 71

O	page
Old House Museum	35, 70
Ollerset	59
One Ash Grange	59
Over Haddon	44, 59
Oxspring	60

P	page
Padley Chapel	26, 49
Padley Wood	17, 55
Paradise Mill	56
Paradise Walk	117
Parkhouse Hill	111
Parsley Hay	112
Parwich	60
Peak Cavern	22, 41, 54, 71, 103
Peak District Lead Mining Museum	
	22, 61, 72
Peak District National Park	12–14, 27–30
Peak Forest	60
Peak Forest Canal	41
Peak Forest Tramway	41
Peak Park Eastern Moors Estate	105
Peak Rail Centre	40
Peakland Eastern Edges	63
Penistone	60–1
Pennine Way	16, 28–9, 46, 48, 65, 74, 96
Peveril Castle	8, 40–1, 71, 103
Pikehall	60
Pilsbury	8, 49
Pilsley	42
Poole's Cavern	22, 40, 70
Priestcliffe	64

R	page
Ramsley Moor	36
reservoirs	50
Riber Castle Wildlife Park	57, 72, 100
riding and trekking	73
Roaches Estate	53, 110
Robin Hood's Picking Rods	59
Robin Hood's Stride	46, 113
Robinson's Moss	65
rock climbing	63
Rowarth	59
Rowsley	44, 61, 72, 98
Rowtor Rocks	37
Roystone Grange	8, 20
Roystone Grange Archaeological Trail	
	60, 114
Rudyard	61
Rushton Spencer	61
Rushup Edge	60

S	page
Saddleworth Moor	57
Saltersford	64
Sett Valley Trail	51, 59, 74
Seven Wonders of the Peak	58
Sheffield	96
Sheldon	22, 61, 108
Sir William Hill	104
Snake Pass	16, 96, 102
Speedwell Cavern	22, 41, 71, 103
Staffordshire Way	61
Stanage	63
Stancliffe Quarry	45
Stanton Moor	7, 37, 62
Stanton in Peak	62
Stocksbridge	62
Stoke Ford	104
Stoney Middleton	62–3

Strines reservoir	38
Surprise View	50
Swythamley Hall	67

T	page
Taddington	64, 98
Tapton House	43
Taxal	64
Temple Mine	22, 72
theatres	75
Thorpe	45
Thorpe Cloud	45
Thor's Cave	53, 54
Three Men of Gardom	105
Throwley	8, 115
Tideswell	8, 25, 54, 64, 98
Tintwistle	65
Tissington	8, 24, 65, 100, 116
Tissington Trail	14, 65, 74, 112, 116
Toad's Mouth Rock	55
Torside reservoir	65, 96
tourist information centres	74–5
Treak Cliff Cavern and Mine	
	34, 41, 71, 103
Trusley	25
Tunstead Quarry	58

U	page
Underbank reservoir	62, 96
Upper Elkstone	66–7
Upper Padley	48

W	page
walking	74
Wardlow	98
Warslow	67
Water-cum-Jolly Dale	55, 107
water-powered mills	44
Waterfall	53
Waterhouses	67
watersports	74
well-dressing	23–4, 54, 65, 116
Wellington Monument	36, 105
Wensley	68
West Bank	68
Wetton	53
Whaley Bridge	64
Wharncliffe Crags	96
Wheel Stones	102
Wheston	64
White Peak	7, 14, 15, 17, 54, 66
Whittington	43
Wigwell aqueduct	44
Wildboarclough	67
wildlife and countryside	15–18
Wincle	67
Windgather Rocks	64
Winnats Pass	41, 103
Winster	68, 100
Wirksworth	8, 26, 68, 72, 100
Woodhead Pass	96
Woodhead tunnels	65
Wormhill	68–9, 98
Wormhill Springs	106
Wortley Top Forge	62
Wye Dale	58

Y	page
Yorkshire Bridge	50
Youlgreave	69, 100

ACKNOWLEDGEMENTS

The Automobile Association wishes to thank the following photographers, libraries
and associations for their assistance in the preparation of this book.

C Daniel 20 Woman Mineworker, 25 Ilam Funeral Garland; *International Photobank* Cover Dove Valley;
Nature Photographers Ltd 16 Ling & Bell Heathers (F V Blackburn), Emperor Moth, Bog Asphodel,
18 Wheatear (P R Sterry); *H Parker* 19 Gollonda Mine, 20 Mr Fox entombed, Standard dish, 21 Lathkill
Dale, Millclose Mine; *Peak National Park* 6 Stannage, 7 Dew Pond, 10/11 Kinder Scout, 11 Notice,
12 Upper Derwent, 15 Dove Valley, 16/17 Cotton Grass, 19 Magpie Mine, 24 Litton Well Dressing,
25 Castleton Garlanding, 26 Rush Bearing, 27 Walking, Ian Hurst, 28 School Party, Briefing Rangers,
29 Ian Hurst, 30 Erecting Footpath signs, 58 Underground river; *J Russell* 16/17 Meadow Cranesbill,
18 Bloody Cranesbill

All remaining pictures are held in the Association's own library (AA Photo Library) with contributions
from: P Baker, M Birkitt, V Greaves, R Newton, A Trynor, T Woodcock.

Ordnance Survey Maps of the Peak District

How to get there with Routemaster and Routeplanner Maps

Reach the Peak District from Lancaster, Newcastle, York, Peterborough, Birmingham and Liverpool
using Routemaster map sheets 5 and 6. Alternatively use the Ordnance Survey Great Britain Routeplanner
Map which covers the whole country on one map sheet.

Exploring with Landranger, Tourist and Outdoor Leisure Maps

Landranger Series
1¼ inches to one mile or 1:50,000 scale.
These maps cover the whole of Britain and are
good for local motoring and walking. Each
contains tourist information such as parking,
picnic places, viewpoints and rights of way.
Sheets covering the Peak District are:
109 Manchester
110 Sheffield and Huddersfield
118 Stoke-on-Trent and Macclesfield
119 Buxton, Matlock and Dovedale

Tourist Map Series
1 inch to one mile or 1:63,360 scale
These maps cover popular holiday areas and are
ideal for discovering the countryside. In addition
to normal map detail ancient monuments,
camping and caravan sites, parking facilities and
viewpoints are marked. Lists of selected places of
interest are included on some sheets and others
include useful guides to the area.

Tourist Map Sheet 4 covers the Peak District

Outdoor Leisure Map Series
2½ inches to one mile or 1:25,000 scale
These maps cover popular leisure and recreation
areas of the country and include details of Youth
Hostels, camping and caravanning sites, picnic
areas, footpaths and viewpoints.

Outdoor Leisure Map Sheets 1 and 24 cover the
Peak District

Other titles available in this series are:
Brecon Beacons; Channel Islands; Cornwall;
Cotswolds; Days out from London; Devon and
Exmoor; East Anglia; Forest of Dean and Wye
Valley; Ireland; Isle of Wight; Lake District; New
Forest; Northumbria; North York Moors; Scottish
Highlands; Snowdonia; South Downs; Wessex;
Yorkshire Dales